At the Science Expo held in Tsukuba in 1985, visitors could write letters to be preserved in a time capsule for 16 years. This New Year's, we received lots of letters from kids (now adults) who were KINNIKUMAN fans back then. In one of those letters, written by a girl, there was this line: "Sixteen years from now, King Muscle and Belinda could be married and have a kid, and maybe that kid could be a wrestler. ♥ "

It-it's like she predicted the creation of this manga...this girl must be Nostradamus!

-Yudetamago

Yudetamago is the pen name of artists Yoshinori Nakai and Takashi Shimada, who created the original hit KINNIKUMAN (MUSCLE MAN). KINNIKUMAN, which debuted in 1979, quickly grew into a massive slapstick wrestling epic and one of the most popular features in Japan's **Weekly Shonen Jump** magazine. ULTIMATE MUSCLE (known in Japan as KINNIKUMAN II SEI) is Yudetamago's most recent creation.

ULTIMATE MUSCLE: BATTLE 14
The SHONEN JUMP ADVANCED Manga Edition

STORY AND ART BY
YUDETAMAGO

Translator/Joe Yamazaki
Touch-up & Lettering/Annaliese Christman
Cover Design & Layout/Izumi Evers
Editor/Shaenon K. Garrity

Managing Editor/Frances E. Wall
Editorial Director/Elizabeth Kawasaki
VP & Editor in Chief/Yumi Hoashi
Sr. Director of Acquisitions/Rika Inouye
Sr. VP of Marketing/Liza Coppola
Exec. VP of Sales & Marketing/John Easum
Publisher/Hyoe Narita

Printed in the U.S.A.

Published by VIZ Media, LLC
P.O. Box 77010
San Francisco, CA 94107

SHONEN JUMP ADVANCED Manga Edition
10 9 8 7 6 5 4 3 2 1
First printing, September 2006

www.viz.com

BATTLE 14

STORY AND ART BY
YUDETAMAGO

BATTLE 14

CONTENTS

CHAPTER 128: DARUMA DOLL OF DOOM

...TO THE STADIUM WHERE TODAY'S EVENT WILL TAKE PLACE!

YEAH

SUPERHUMAN OLYMPICS THE RESURRECTION

FA LA LA LA LA LA...

HE'S TOTALLY OFF-KEY!

UGH... I'VE NEVER HEARD A NASTIER SINGING VOICE...

LALA

LALALALA

...THAT HAUNTS YO NIGHT AND DAY...

THANKS FOR LISTENING!
CLAP
CLAP
CLAP
LA LA LA LA
!
SWANEE
WHO CHANGED THE DISC?
FA LA LA LA

TRA LA LA
ME!

WAY DOWN UPON THE SWANEE RIVER...

UP AHEAD IS THE STAGE FOR YOUR NEXT EVENT...
SUPERHUMAN OLYMPICS
SUPERHUMAN OLYMPICS
...CHIBA MARINE STADIUM!

ATTEN-TION, SUPER-HUMANS!
WE ARE NOW ENTERING CHIBA'S MAKUHARI MESSE AREA.
SHF

LOVE LIKE MEN
HERE WE ARE AT CHIBA MARINE STADIUM!
TODAY, IN THE HIGH-TECH TOWN OF MAKUHARI MESSE...
...THE NEXT EVENT OF THE SUPERHUMAN OLYMPICS IS ABOUT TO TAKE PLACE!
THE CAPACITY CROWD HERE AT MARINE STADIUM HAS BEEN WAITING WITH BATED BREATH!
WAAAA
YOUNG SUPERHUMANS! AS YOU ALL KNOW, THE SUPERHUMAN OLYMPICS...
...IS A COLD AND HEARTLESS GAME OF SURVIVAL TO DECIDE THE WORLD'S NUMBER-ONE SUPERHUMAN!

BINK

DARUMA OTOSHI BAM!

papasonic

...DARUMA DOLLS!*

**DARUMA OTOSHI*: A TRADITIONAL JAPANESE CHILDREN'S TOY. KIDS USE A HAMMER TO KNOCK BLOCKS OUT FROM UNDER A WOODEN *DARUMA* DOLL.

CLICK

RUMBLE

OH! THE STADIUM TREMBLES WITH AN INCREDIBLE ROAR AND RUMBLE!

RMM

RM

M

RMM

WH-WHAT'S GOING ON?

LOOK! TWO TOWERS RISING FROM THE GROUND!
WHAT THE--
GRM

IT'S A
GIANT
DARUMA
OTOSHI
TOY!

SO WE'RE
GONNA PLAY
USING THIS
HUGE
TOWER?
ACT-
LY!

ER...
YOU
CAN GO
FIRST!

THIS SPECIAL
DARUMA DOLL
WAS CARVED
FROM A SINGLE
BLOCK OF
STONE...
...BY
FIRST-RATE
STONEMASONS,
TAKING OVER
A MONTH TO
COMPLETE.

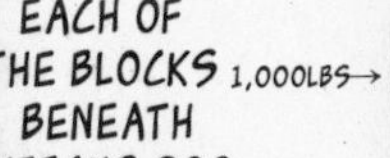
IT'S
DIVIDED
INTO FIVE
PIECES.
THE HEAD
WEIGHS
1,000
POUNDS.
EACH OF
HE BLOCKS
BENEATH
EIGHS 900
POUNDS.
THE TOTAL
WEIGHT
OF THE
TOWER
IS 4,600
POUNDS.
1,000LBS →
900LBS →
900LBS →
900LBS →
900LBS →
2
3
4
5

HE
WHO CAN
REMOVE
ALL FOUR
BLOCKS...
..WITHOUT
TOPPLING
THE HEAD
WILL WIN.
2
4
5

BUT THERE'S N
HAMMER, AS THERE IS IN NORMAL DARUMA OTOSHI.
I WANT YOU TO REMOVE THE BLOCKS USING ONLY YOUR BODIES!
4,600 POUNDS... THAT'S OVER TWO TONS! AND WE CAN ONLY USE OUR BODIES?
WHAT A GRUELING COMPETITION...

NICE! "WICKED DARUMA DOLLS"! I'M GETTING PUMPED UP...
KRIK KRAK
HA! AFTER THE LAST ROUND, I DIDN'T KNOW WHAT TO EXPECT...
...BUT THIS IS MORE LIKE THE SUPERHUMAN OLYMPICS!

IRAQ'S GENOCIDE AND TURKEY'S OTTOMAN HAV
VOLUNTEERED...
...TO BE THE FIRST TWO CHALLENGERS FOR THIS ROUND!
CLAP CLAP CLAP
HOW COURAGEOUS OF THEM!

AND NOW THE SECOND EVENT...

...DARUMA OTOSHI BAM... WILL BEGIN!

HEH... THIS'LL BE A CINCH!

OH! IRAQ'S GENO-CIDE...

...UNLEASHES A LIGHTNING-QUICK MIDDLE KICK TO THE DARUMA TOWER!

HAS HE SUCCEEDED IN REMOVING ONE OF THE BLOCKS?
GYAAA!
M-MY LEG!!
SNAP
THE STONE TOWER DOESN'T BUDGE!
INSTEAD, GENOCIDE'S KICKING LEG SNAPS IN HALF!

HO HO HO! THAT'S WHAT YOU GET FOR ENTERING THE SUPERHUMAN OLYMPICS WITHOUT HAVING ANY REAL SKILL!
GYAAAA
EVERYBODY WATCH ME! THIS HOW A CHAMPION DOES IT!
WMP
THE SECOND CHALLENGER, OTTOMAN, ATTEMPTS TO REMOVE THE BLOCKS WITH HIS FIST!
GURAAAA!
WHAM
KRK
KRK
ARRGH!

READ THIS WAY

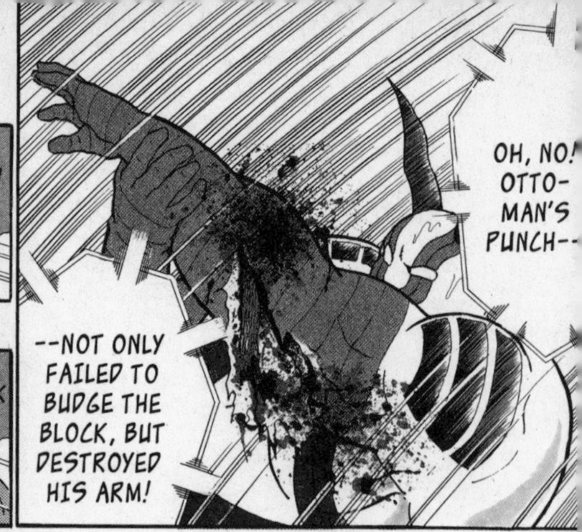

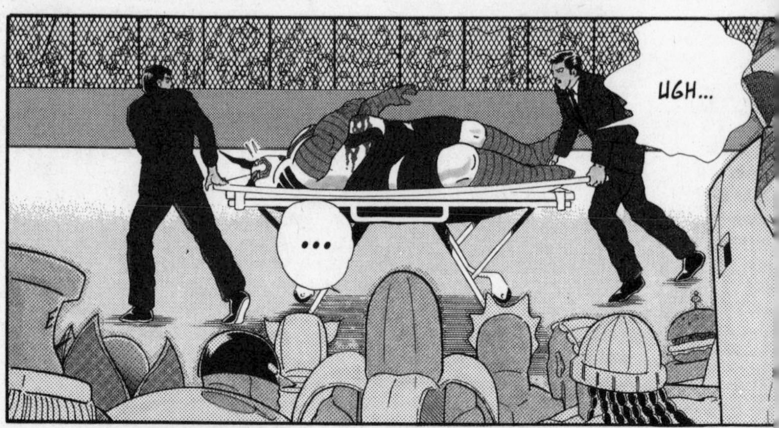

THE THIRD CHALLENGER IS WALLY TUSKET OF IRELAND!

TMP

WALLY TUSKET'S WICKED DARUMA DOLL CHALLENGE IS ABOUT TO BEGIN!

WALLY!

C'MON WALLY

I KNOW YOU CAN DO IT!

BELIEVE IN YOURSELF. BACK IN IRELAND...

...YOU TOOK DOWN WHALES WITH ONLY YOUR KICK.

YEAH

ALL RIGHT! HERE I GO!

AARGH!

SWUP

WALLY TUSKE KICKS OUT THE THIRD BLOCK OF TH DARUMA TOWER!

NICE!

THMP

TAK

TAK

BUT THE REMAINING BLOCKS ARE TEETERING DANGEROUSLY!

TUK
WALLY!
WALLY!
!
GRM
GRM
GRM
GRM
AUGH!

CHAPTER 129: A DESPERATE CHEER

THE BLOCKS OF THE DARUMA TOWE WEIGHING TWO TONS...

...FALL MERCILESSLY ON WALLY TUSKET!

WALLY!

IRELAND'S WALLY TUSKET, ONE OF THE FIRST GRADUATES OF THE HERCULES FACTORY, WHO WAS THOUGHT TO BE A SHOO-IN...

...MAKES AN EARLY EXIT!

NEXT CHAL-LENGER.

WHAT A BUNCH OF WIMPS!
BACK IN MY DAY, THE SUPER-HUMAN OLYMPICS WAS A PLACE...
SQK SQK
...TO MAKE A NAME FOR YOURSELF AT ANY COST!

GO AHEAD!

MUSCL BOY'S SUCH WUSS!
IT'D BE SO COOL IF HE STEPPED UP RIGHT NOW.

NOT ALL YOUNG SUPERHUMANS ARE GUTLESS!

KEVIN MASK!
SH-
HOW
FF?
IT LOOKS LIKE BRITAIN'S KEVIN MASK IS GOING TO TRY HIS LUCK!
BUT NO MATTER HOW SKILLED WE ARE...
...WE DON'T SHOW OFF LIKE YOU OLD MEN USED TO!
SHK
SHK
HE'S GOT THAT RIGHT!

TERRY KENYON'S GONNA TRY IT!

TERRY! NO WAY!

SHK

WE FIGHT WITH A QUIET SPIRIT OF OUR OWN! THAT'S THE NEW GENERATION

SHK

YOU TALK BIG...

...BUT LET'S SEE IF THE NEW GENERATION HAS WHAT IT TAKES!

I-I DON'T CARE IF I'M NOT COOL.

I'D RATHER SAVE MY SKIN...

KEVIN MASK AND TERRY KENYON, A DREAM COMBO, WILL ATTEMPT THE DARUMA TOWER!

THEY'RE SO COOL!

THAT'S HOW A MAN SHOULD BE!

YOU MAY HAVE THE HONORS. I WANT TO SEE YOUR SO-CALLED TEXAS SPIRIT!
YOU BET!
2
3
4
5
2
3
4
5
PAF PAF
LOOKS LIKE ERRY KENYON IS READY!
RGH--
DASH
TERRY AUNCHES...
GRRR
RAARGH!

3
OH! HE BRILLIANTLY CHOPS OUT THE BLOCK!
...A FLYING CROSS CHOP TO THE THIRD BLOCK!
SHAKK
3
4
5
GAK
2
GAK
GAK
SHP
DOK
HI-YA!

GAK

HE CLEARS THE FOURTH BLOCK!

OH--BUT THE UPPER BLOCKS LOSE THEIR BALANCE!

THEY'RE FALLING TOWARD TERRY KENYON!

YAH!

DOK

SEE? WHAT'D I TELL YOU?

YAH!
WHAM
THUD
TERRY KENYON SUCCEEDS!
WAA
AMERICA'S TERRY KENYON...
...IS THE FIRST TO CLEAR "DARUMA OTOSHI BAM"!
YES!
HMPH... YOUR PERFORMANCE WAS LAUDABLE.
HUH? TERRY DID IT?
BUT IT WAS TOO ROUGH AROUND THE EDGES.

HUA!
KEVIN MASK FOLLOWS WITH A HEAVY LOW KICK...
W
THE TOP BLOCKS HOVER FOR AN INSTANT--
2
3
4
DAH
III--
A
K
...KNOCKING OUT THE FIFTH BLOCK OF THE DARUMA TOWER!
--YAH!
WAK
HUA!
WAK
--AND HE SKILLFULLY KICKS OUT THE SECOND AND THIRD BLOCKS!

T
HE BLOWS OUT THE LAST BLOCK WITH A ROLLING SOBUT!
LAST ONE!
HUK
WHAT PRECISE KICKS!
WHOA...
TAK
WHAM
KEVIN MASK HAS CLEARED THE SECOND EVENT!
KEVIN MASK DIDN'T JUST KICK OUT THE BLOCKS...
...HE STACKED THEM ON TOP OF EACH OTHER!

OH, KEVIN!

YEAH!

...

AH...

BA
LET'S SEE YOU RUN AWAY NOW!
HUH? ROX-ANNE?
ROX-ANNE!
HOLY COW!
WHAT'S THIS? OUT OF NOWHERE...
...A GIRL HAS JUMPED ONTO THE DARUMA TOWER!
TAK
WHOA

NO! WHAT ARE YOU DOING, ROXANNE?
DAH
ALL RIGHT! THE NEXT CHAL-LENGER!
WHAT? NO!
I WAS JUST TRYING TO HELP ROXANNE...
C'MON! PLEASE GET HER OFF THAT THING!
2
3
4
5
THIS TOURN-AMENT IS SCHEDULED DOWN TO THE LAST SECOND!
WE DON'T HAVE TIME TO RESCUE SOME GIRL!
AN OLYMPI
YIKES!
SLP
ROXANNE!

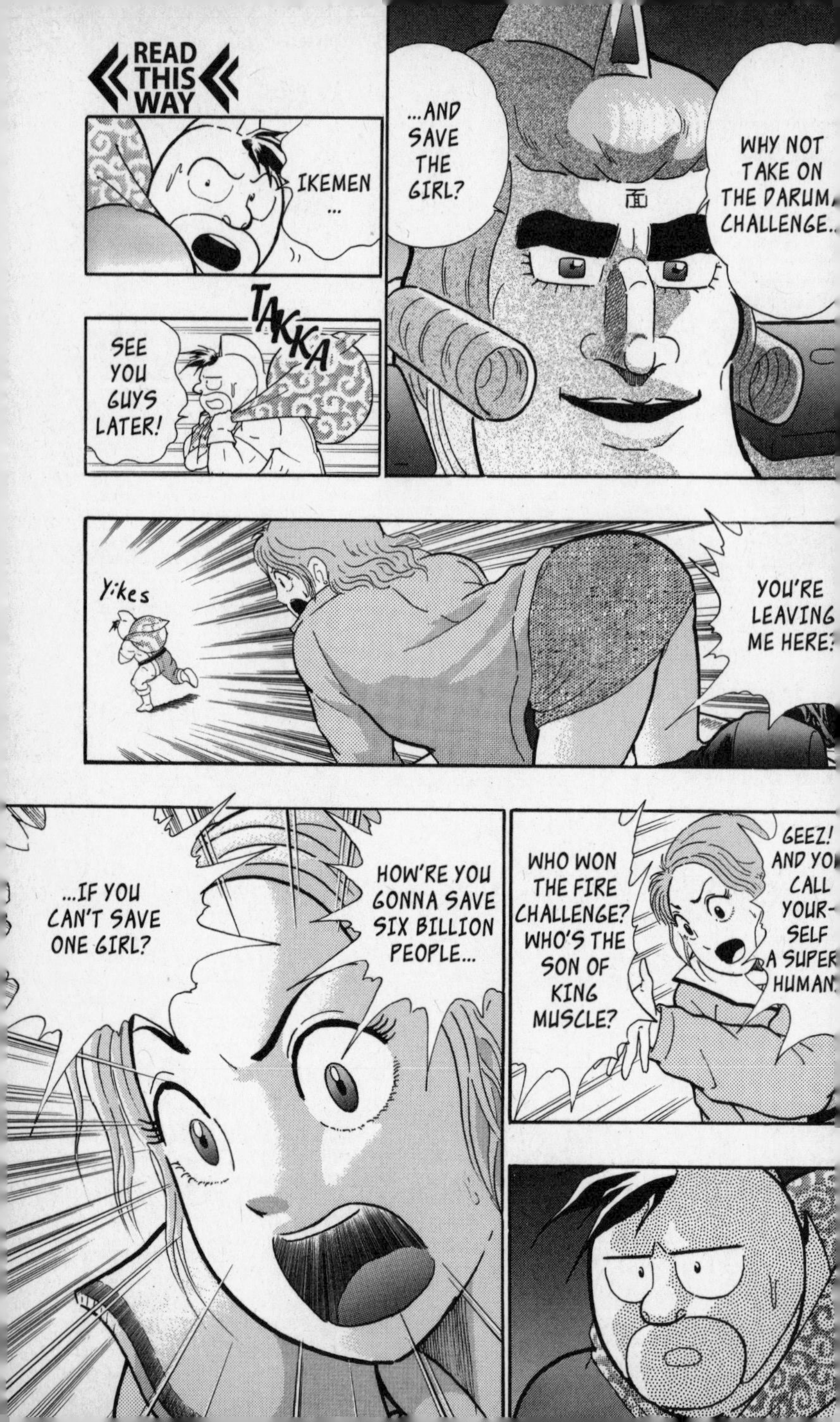

READ THIS WAY

WHY NOT TAKE ON THE DARUMA CHALLENGE...

...AND SAVE THE GIRL?

IKEMEN...

TAKKA

SEE YOU GUYS LATER!

YOU'RE LEAVING ME HERE!?

Yikes

GEEZ! AND YOU CALL YOURSELF A SUPER HUMAN.

WHO WON THE FIRE CHALLENGE? WHO'S THE SON OF KING MUSCLE?

HOW'RE YOU GONNA SAVE SIX BILLION PEOPLE...

...IF YOU CAN'T SAVE ONE GIRL?

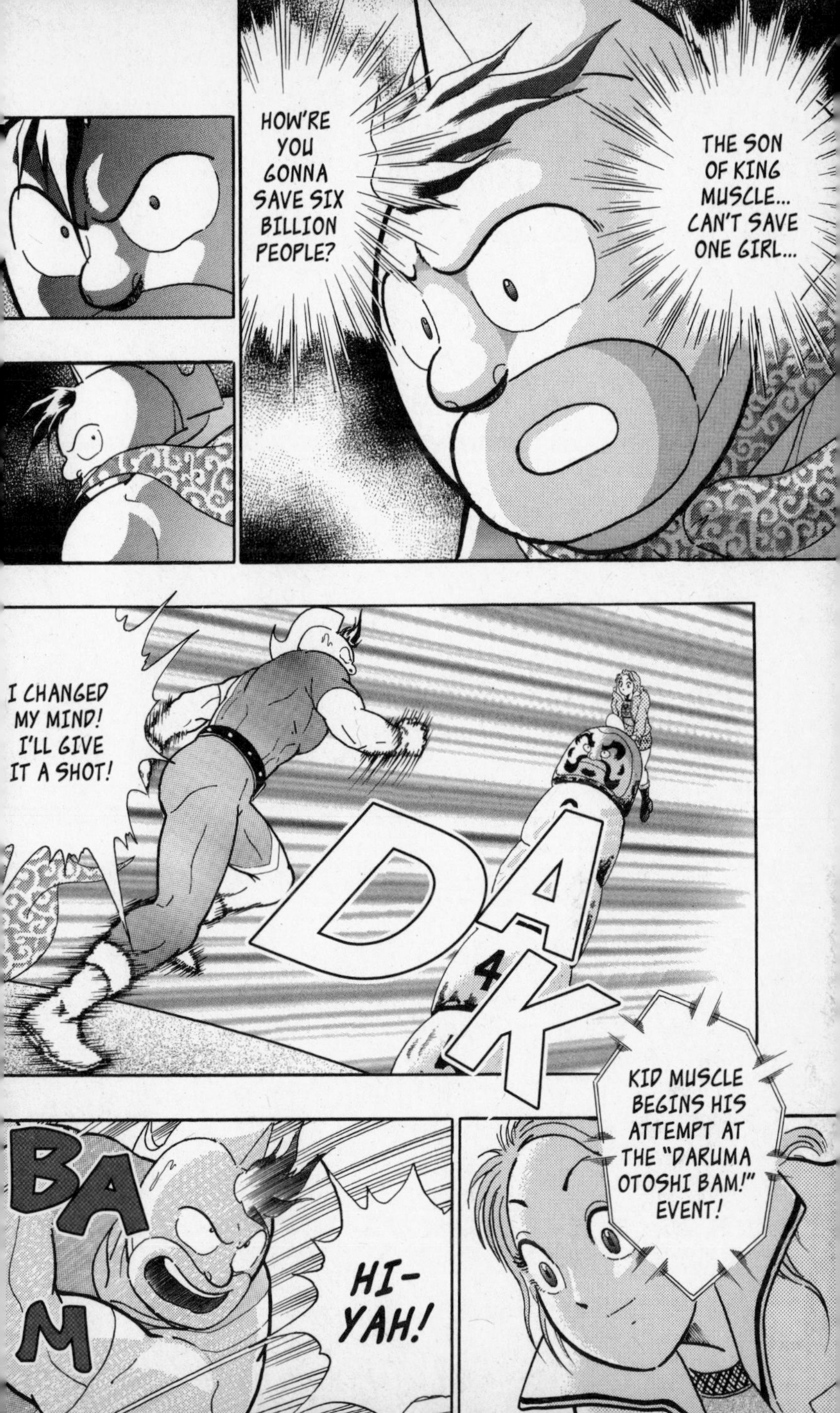
THE SON OF KING MUSCLE... CAN'T SAVE ONE GIRL...
HOW'RE YOU GONNA SAVE SIX BILLION PEOPLE?
DAK
I CHANGED MY MIND! I'LL GIVE IT A SHOT!
KID MUSCLE BEGINS HIS ATTEMPT AT THE "DARUMA OTOSHI BAM!" EVENT!
HI-YAH!
BAM

TH
UK
IT'S UNEVEN, BUT HE SUCCEEDS IN REMOVING ONE BLOCK!
2
GAK
YEEK!
HE LANDS A ROLLING SOBUT ON THE THIRD BLOCK!
ROXANNE!
THUD
KID MUSCLE REMOVES THE FOURTH BLOCK WITH A HIP ATTACK!
DOK
TH-THAT HURT!

WHOA!

BUT IT'S ONLY A MATTER OF TIME BEFORE THE TOWER FALLS, TAKING THE GIRL WITH IT!

WHOOPS!

SLIP

YES! NOW MAN-TARO'S DISQUALIFIED FOR SURE!

WHAT'S THIS? WITHOUT USING HIS ARMS OR LEGS...
FWAP
...KID MUSCLE KNOCKS THE BLOCKS ASIDE WITH LIGHTNING SPEED!
FWAP
2
5
EEK!
AND THE HEAD FALLS!
ZOOM

OH! I DON'T KNOW WHAT JUST HAPPENED, BUT KID MUSCLE OF JAPAN...

...SURVIVES THE SECOND EVENT!

WHAT WAS THAT?

CHAPTER 130:
RESCUE OR DIE!
THE CHARACTERS IN CHAPTER 126 WERE BASED ON IDEAS FROM THE FOLLOWING READERS:
MISTER SHIP — TAKASHI WATANABE (27)
GENOCIDE — YASUSHI OKABE (25)
THE CUTTER MAOH — KENTARO SAKAMOTO (14)
TORNADO FAN — YUICHIRO ATAMI (28)
THE DIE-OXIN — HUMIHIKO ISHIZAWA (24)
THE COASTERMAN — DAISUKE USHIMARU (20)
THANK YOU FOR YOUR SUBMISSIONS.
IT FIRST APPEARED AS IF NO ONE WOULD CLEAR...
...THE BRUTAL "DARUMA OTOSHI BAM!" CHALLENGE!

WHAK

CHIJIMIMAN: PASS!

THUK

THE SENSATION: PASS!

WHIP

CLICK
IO IO
W.C
HOLLYWOOD BOWL!
PSSH
PSSH
AND NOW FOR THE FINAL CHALLENGER IN THIS ROUND!
BAAAM
JAEGAR, REPRE-SENTING GERMANY, WILL MAKE THE ATTEMPT!
STUP
STUP

RED RAIN!
JAEGER TAKES OUT TWO BLOCKS AT ONCE!
JAEGER: PASS!
OUT OF THE 260 PARTICIPANTS IN THE SECOND EVENT, 65 FAILED.
THE REMAINING 195 SUPER-HUMANS WILL MOVE ON TO THE THIRD EVENT!
Y-YOU'LL FAIL THE NEXT EVENT...
...FOR CERTAIN!

THE NEXT DAY...
SHUU
HERE WE ARE AT KANAGAWA'S SHONAN BEACH!
SUPERHUMAN OLYMPICS THE RESURRECTION
WAAAA
SURFERS USUALLY CROWD THIS BEACH...
...BUT TODAY IT WILL BE THE STAGE OF BATTLE FOR THE SUPERHUMAN OLYMPICS!

YEEK... I CAN'T SWIM!
SHF
I'M GONNA RUSTLE UP SOME SEAFOOD ...

I KNOW IT'S BEEN A HOT SUMMER, BUT I HOPE THEY DON'T GIVE US A SWIMMING COMPETITION.

THE COMPETITION'S ABOUT TO START!
YANK
I NOW!

AND NOW THE TOURNAMENT CHAIRMAN, MR. IKEMEN MCMADD...
...WILL EXPLAIN HE RULES OF THE THIRD EVENT!
KID LOVE

DON'T WORRY!
WE WON'T THROW YOU IN THE WATER!

WHEW!
風神
北海道

THE THIRD EVENT...
...WILL TAKE PLACE ON THE VAST BEACH...
...BENEATH YOUR FEET!
THE THIRD EVENT IN THE SUPER-HUMAN OLYMPICS IS...
KEZOE HEAD STORE
EPNSO
BEACH FLAGS YEAH!
"BEACH FLAGS YEAH!"
WHOA...
HUH? BEACH FRANKEN-STEIN?

"BEACH FLAGS" STARTED AS A DRILL FOR LIFEGUARDS.
THEN IT TURNED INTO A BEACH SPORT.

A FLAG IS STUCK IN THE SAND.
THE PLAYERS LIE DOWN T ONE END OF THE BEACH.

AT THE SIGNAL, THEY RACE ...
...TO GRAB THE FLAG!
HUH? IT'S JUST RACING FOR A FLAG?
OH, THAT'S EASY!
I DON'T MIND GOING FIRST!
Fight
THE COMPE-TITION WILL TAKE PLACE JUST AS ERRY KENYON DESCRIBED.

CLICK
STA
SPLASH
GOA
ZHA

A SPECIAL TRACK HAS SUDDENLY RISEN FROM UNDER THE BEACH!
GOA
SUPERHUMAN OLYMPICS THE RESURRECTION
OKAY, SO THAT'S THE TRACK...
START

GOAL
SUPERHUMAN OLYMPICS THE RESURRECTION
HEY, THERE'S NO FLAG AT THE GOAL!
OH, I'VE ARRANGED FOR A FLAG...
...TRULY WORTHY OF THE SUPER HUMAN OLYMPICS.
PEEP

GOAL
AAAHN
OH! SOMETHING LIKE A DEMON OR A DEVIL...
WM
...HAS SUDDENLY EMERGED, WITH A FACE OF OTHERWORLDLY HORROR!
WWMMWWMM

HA HA HA! THAT'S THE SPECIAL FLAG FOR THIS COMPETITION

THAT HIDEOUS MASK REPRESENTS AN EVIL SUPERHUMAN...

EEEEEE

...WHO HAS JUST ATTACKED AN INNOCENT WOMAN!

AT THE SIGNAL, THE MASK WILL DROP THE WOMAN FROM ITS MOUTH.

THREE SUPERHUMANS WILL RACE TO CATCH HER. THE ONE WHO SUCCEEDS WILL ADVANCE TO THE NEXT ROUND!

OF COURSE!

WHAT O YOU MEAN, "OF OURSE"?

READ THIS WAY

...THINK OF ALL THE NEGATIVE PUBLICITY!

YOU KILLER!
THAT GUY LET SOMEBODY *DIE!*

UGH!

IF THAT HAPPEN- YOU'LL NEVER B ABLE TO LEAVE TH HOUSE.
OF COURSE, PARTYING AND HITTING ON GIRLS WILL BE OUT OF THE QUESTION.

ER... I DON'T *HAVE* TO GO FIRST...

GET OFF THE PLANET YOU USELES SUPERHUMA
WE DON'T NEED YOU, IDIOT!
HMPH. COWARD.

WE'VE PRE-ARRANGED THE GROUPINGS FOR THIS EVENT.
WHEN YOUR NAME IS CALLED, PLEASE APPROACH THE STARTING LINE!
SAUDI ARABIA'S POWER-MAN!
FLEX
YEAH!
ZAK
NORWAY'S GHOST VIKING!
GRRR!
SWEDEN'S BARRIER-FREEMAN!
HO HO HO!

THE FIRST GROUP NOW STANDS AT THE STARTIN LINE.
I'M PREDICTING BARRIER-FREEMAN WILL BE OUTCLASSED BY THE OTHER TWO!
GOAL
SUPERHUMAN OLYMPICS THE RESURRECTION
START
HEADS DOWN!
ALL THREE LIE FACE DOWN!
READY ... GET SET...
POK
THE MOUTH OF THE EVIL MASK OPENS!
BANG
GO!
DAK
DAK
DAK

AT THE SOUND OF THE SIGNAL GUN...
...POWERMAN AND GHOST VIKING START OFF, NECK AND NECK!
DASH
IT'LL BE A RACE BETWEEN THESE TWO!
WAIT! WHAT'S
APPENING
...
TAK
HYO!
TO BARRIER-FREEMAN?
HE
AKES ON
HE SHAPE
OF AN
LD MAN!
KA
TAK
HE'S FAST! HE'S FAST!
ARRIERFREEMAN CATCHES UP IN NO TIME!
KAK
HYO!

OH-- BUT THE WOMAN IS ABOUT TO FALL TO THE GROUND!
SUPERHUMAN OLYMPICS THE RESURRECTION
WHOA!
BOP
WHOA!
BOP
HO!
TAKKA
NYO HO HO!
THE OLD MAN TACKLES THE COMPETITION!
WUP

BARRIER-FREEMAN SAFELY CATCHES THE WOMAN...
SHUCK
...AND EARNS A TICKET TO THE FOURTH EVENT!
WAA
WHAT A MOVE!
EEEK!!
HYO... HYO...
I LOVE YOUNG GIRLS!
HEY! WHAT THE HELL ARE OU DOING?
LET'S MOVE ON! NEXT GROUP, PLEASE!
LIBYA'S MEAN MARINE!

YEAH
ABOU
TIME
THD
THD
RUSSIA
COMRA
TURBINS
ZAK
ZAK
ALGERIA'S MAD PENGUIN!

EEK! HELP!

THE EVIL MASK HAS A DIFFERENT WOMAN IN ITS MOUTH!

HEADS DOWN!

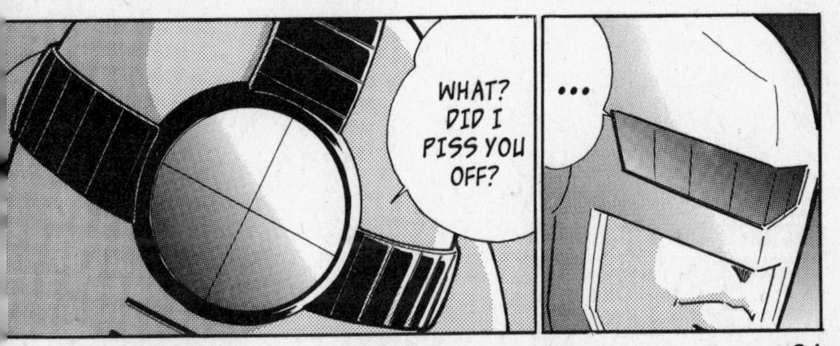

CHAPTER 131:
WHAT DO HEROES CHOOSE?

THESE THREE SUPERHUMAN POWERHOUSES EAGERLY AWAIT THE SIGNAL TO RUN!

THE SUPERHUMANS APPEARING IN THIS CHAPTER WERE BASED ON IDEAS FROM THE FOLLOWING PEOPLE:

KOUTARO MARUYAMA (21) IBARAKI
KENJI OOYAMA (28) SAITAMA
KINKETSU-MAN (23) FUKUI
KENTARO SAKAMOTO (17) OSAKA
YOSHITATSU NISHINAKA (25) OSAKA

THANK YOU FOR YOUR SUBMISSIONS!

THE SECOND GROUP FOR THE "BEACH FLAGS YEAH!" EVENT INCLUDES MEAN MARINE, COMRADE TURBINSKI AND MAD PENGUIN!

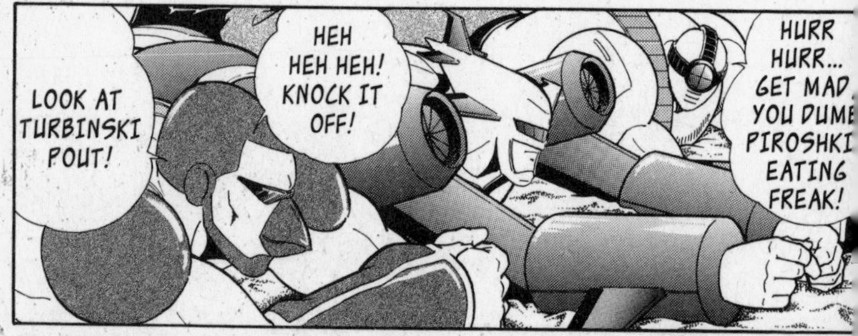

...
THEY'RE TRYING TO PSYCH COMRADE TURBINSKI OUT.
I HOPE HE DOESN'T FALL FOR IT AND LOSE HIS COOL.
EEK!
THE BEAUTIFUL GIRL IN THE ATHING SUIT IS FALLING FROM THE MOUTH OF THE MASK!
READY ... GET SET...
BANG
GO!
DAKK
AT THE SIGNAL, THE THREE SUPERHUMANS SPRING INTO ACTION!
A
TO SAVE THE FALLING GIRL...
...THEY RUN ONTO THE TRACK TOGETHER!
READY?
EAH!

GO!

GSSH

OH! MEAN MARINE AND MAD PENGUIN HAVE COLLUDED!

THEY'RE BOTH ELBOWING COMRADE TURBINSKI!

SHK

STAY DOWN, YOU PILE OF JUNK!

OUR ALLIANCE IS OVER, MAD PENGUIN.

SEE YOU LATER!

DAK

TRAITOR!

UGH...

BAH
AIRCRAFT GENETICS!
WOOSH
DEATH-MAMA RIOT!
WHOOOM
SO THAT'S COMRADE TURBINSKI'S BIG MOVE!
WHOA!
ING
6 17 23
4 20 24
15
風神
北京

CRUNCH
NOO!
OH, NO! COMRADE TURBINSKI'S WING SLICES OFF MAD PENGUIN'S HEAD!
WHY, YOU..
DOK
COMMANDO SHELL!
FOOOM
SLUK
MEAN MARINE, RUNNING AHEAD, FIRES AN IRON BALL FROM THE CANNON ON HIS BACK!
UGH...

ZAAK
GAUGH!
BUT THE MURDEROUS WING SLICES INTO MEAN MARINE AS WELL!
WHILE THEY BATTLE, THE GIRL IS ABOUT TO SLAM INTO THE GROUND!
SHAING
SHAK
EEK!

ZHAK
COMRADE TURBINSK SAVES TH GIRL WIT A LAST-SECOND DIVE!
COMRADE TURBINSKI: PASS!
THIS MUSCLE LEAGUE FESTIVAL HAS TAKEN AN UNEXPECTEDLY GHASTLY TURN!

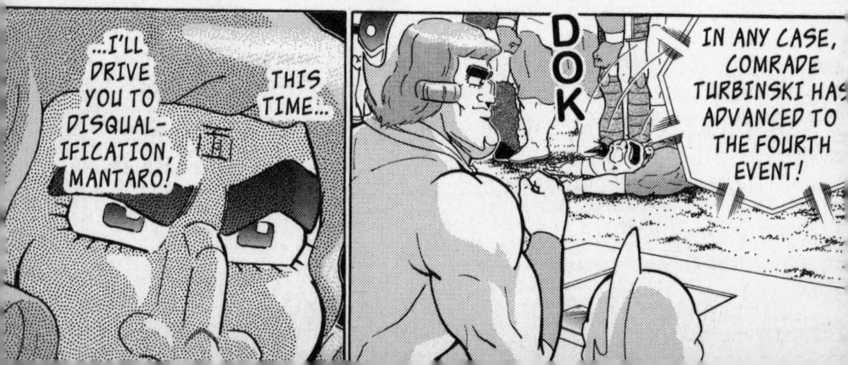

THE COMPETITION CONTINUED.

SUPERHUMANS WHO PERFORMED BEST IN SOLO COMPETITIONS...

...HAD TROUBLE IN AN EVENT WHERE TWO OUT OF THREE ENTRANTS WERE DISQUALIFIED.

THE MENTAL TOUGHNESS REQUIRED TO SURVIVE COMPETITORS' DEMORALIZING TACTICS...

...AND THE ABILITY TO COME THROUGH IN A PINCH SEPARATED THE WINNERS FROM THE LOSERS.

OW OW...
HOO BOY...
THE 54TH GROUPING!
Fight!
b-dmp b-dmp
PLEASE DON'T LET IT BE ME...
JAPAN'S KID MUSCLE.
TWITCH
NYO NYO NYO!
CANADA'S BOBBY WASABI!
TAIWAN'S MR. PEEL!
YES!

GOOD LUCK!

GOAL

START

GAA

WHOA!

MYO MYO MYO MYO

A NEW HUMAN SACRIFICE HAS BEEN PLACED IN THE EVIL MASK'S MOUTH!
I STAYED UP ALL NIGHT TO COME UP WITH THE ULTIMATE ANTI-MANTARO LINEUP!
GOAL
WHAT KIND OF GIRL IS IT GONNA BE THIS TIME?
I HOPE SHE'S STACKED!
OH! THE NEW SACRIFICIAL VICTIM IS...
EEK!
BOING
...A FAT GUY IN A LOINCLOTH!
WHAT?
HEY! WHY DON'T WE GET A BIKINI BABE?

I TOLD YOU, THIS EVENT IS MEANT TO SIMULATE...

...A HUMAN BEING ATTACKED BY AN EVIL SUPERHUMAN!

IN THE REAL WORLD, EVILDOERS DON'T JUST ATTACK PRETTY GIRLS!

THEY TTACK 'S, OLD OPLE...

... EVEN FAT, GREASY ...

ALD DDLE- GED EN!

WHEN FACED WITH THAT SITUATION, WILL YOU REFUSE TO RESCUE HIM, MANTARO?

JUST BECAUSE HE'S A MAN?

WELL, ER...

MUSCLE LEAGUE CHAMPIONS MAKE NO DISTINCTION BETWEEN THE NEEDY!

YOU MUST SAVE *EVERYONE* ON THE PLANET!

OKAY, OKAY! I'LL RESCUE CUEBALL UP THERE!

EADS WN!

START

GEEZ... NOT ONLY AM I GROUPED WITH THES SCARY DUDES, I'VE GOTTA SAVE AN OLD MAN!
THIS HAS TO BE IKEMEN'S DOING!
READY ... GET SET ...
THE OLD MAN HAS JUST DROPPED!
EEE...
BANG
GO!
AND NOW THE 54TH GROUP HAS MADE ITS START!
DADAKK
START
TAKING THE LEAD IS TAIWAN'S MR. PEEL!
SURPRIS INGLY, JAPAN'S KID MUSCLE...
DAK DAK
DAK DAK
...IS IN 2ND PLACE, RIGHT BEHIND MR. PEEL!
GO MAN-TARO!
PASS HIM, PASS HIM!
MAN-TARO!
DAK

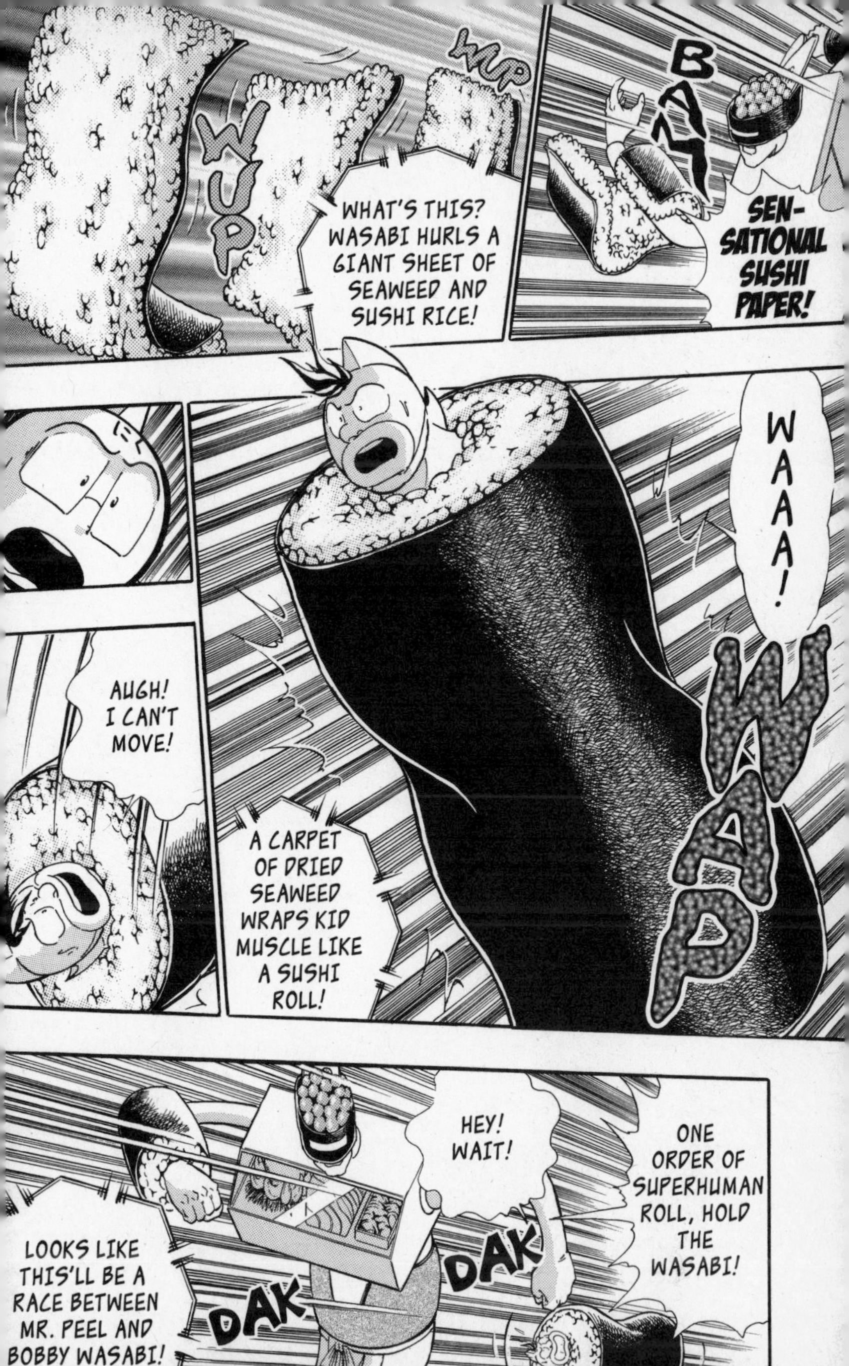
WUP
WUP
BAM
SEN-SATIONAL SUSHI PAPER!
WHAT'S THIS? WASABI HURLS A GIANT SHEET OF SEAWEED AND SUSHI RICE!
WAAAA!
WAP
AUGH! I CAN'T MOVE!
A CARPET OF DRIED SEAWEED WRAPS KID MUSCLE LIKE A SUSHI ROLL!
ONE ORDER OF SUPERHUMAN ROLL, HOLD THE WASABI!
HEY! WAIT!
DAK
DAK
LOOKS LIKE THIS'LL BE A RACE BETWEEN MR. PEEL AND BOBBY WASABI!

DAK
NYA HA HA! BOBBY WASABI
...YOUR EFFORTS END HERE!
DAK
BANANA PEEL!
SLP
PEEL
MR. PEEL PEELS OFF A PORTION OF HIS COSTUME!
HE DROPS IT IN BOBBY WASABI'S LANE!
TUP
NYOOO!
SL
UP
OH! BOBBY WASABI...
...SLIPS ON THE BANANA PEEL AND FALLS!
UGH!

WITH HIS RIVALS ELIMINATED, MR. PEEL IS SECONDS FROM VICTORY!
DA KA KK
GOAL
I'M STILL HERE!
STILL WRAPPED IN A SUSHI ROLL...
BOING BOING BOING
YOU'LL NEVER MAKE IT!
THIS RACE IS MINE!
YES! GO!
GO!
...KID MUSCLE IS GAINING GROUND, ONE HOP AT A TIME!
WAIT!

--BUT HE KEEPS FLYING FORWARD!

GOAL

MR. PEEL IS ALMOST AT THE FINISH LINE!

GOAL

GRAB
KID MUSCLE: PASS!
YES!
WAA
JAPAN'S KID MUSCLE ONCE AGAIN PULLS OF A MIRACULOUS VICTORY FROM BEHIND, ADVANCING TO THE NEXT EVENT.
SO... HEAVY...
SUPERHUMAN
THE RESURRECTION
NEXT UP IS THE 55TH GROUPING ...
MR. PEEL, YOU IDIOT! HOW COULD YOU?

GREECE'S BARONUS!

EAH!

SIR!

GERMANY'S JAEGER!

TUP

OH, NO! TERRY KENYON AND JAEGER WILL BE COMPETING!

NPIC

CHAPTER 132: THE TERRY FAMILY SPIRIT

WHAT A TWIST OF FATE! THE NEXT QUALIFYING MATCH...

...PITS TERRY KENYON AGAINST JAEGER!

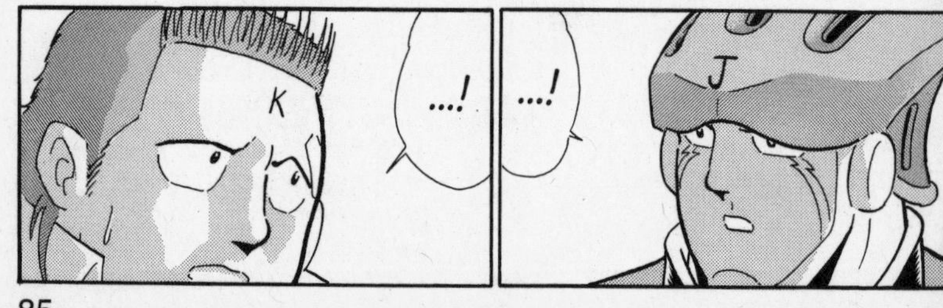

THIS MATCHUP WOULDN'T BE A SURPRISE IN THE SUPERHUMAN OLYMPICS FINALS!
UT TO SEE IT IN
E QUALIFIERS...
THIS CAN ONLY
HAPPEN IN THE
SUPERHUMAN
LYMPICS, WHERE
HE WORLD'S TOP
SUPERHUMANS
GATHER!

LET'S GIVE IT OUR BEST!

JA!

WITH THIS GOLDEN MATCHUP NOW A REALITY, THE CROWD ERUPTS IN CHEERS!

TERRY TERRY

TERRY! TERRY!

JAEGER! JAEGER!

JAEGER! JAEGER!

TERRY KENYON'S FATHER, THE LEGENDARY TERRYMAN, FINISHED THIRD IN THE 1980 SUPERHUMAN OLYMPICS.

THE FOLLOWING YEAR, HE WAS ELIMINATED IN THE QUALIFIERS. HE HAS NEVER BEEN CHAMPION.

JAEGER'S TRAINER, BROCKEN JR., IS ANOTHER LEGENDARY WRESTLER.

HE PARTICIPATED IN THE 1981 SUPERHUMAN OLYMPICS, BUT HE WAS ELIMINATED IN THE SECOND ROUND.

IN OTHER WORDS, TERRY KENYON AND JAEGER...

...ARE BOTH DETERMINED TO WIN THE VICTORY THAT ESCAPED THEIR PREDECESSORS!

READ THIS WAY

KID
TERRY!
TERRY!

JAEGER!
JAEGER!

AW, MAN! TERRY KENYON'S COOL, BUT SO IS JAEGER!
I DON'T KNOW WHO TO CHEER FOR!

BARONUS!
BARONUS!
SUPPORTERS FOR BARONUS, WHO IS COMPETING AGAINST TERRY KENYON AND JAEGER, TRY NOT TO BE OUTCHEERED!

PERHAPS THIS REPRESENTATIV FROM GREECE, WHERE THE OLYMPICS ORIGINATED, CAN DEFEAT BOTH KENYON AND JAEGER!
BARONUS!
BARONUS!
BARONUS!

JAEGER!
JAEGER!
TERRY! TERRY!
BARONUS!
BARONUS!

ANY ONE OF THESE THREE CAN WIN!

NOW GERMANY'S JAEGER AND GREECE'S BARONUS CONSULT THEIR COACHES...

...FOR FINAL WORDS OF ADVICE BEFORE THE BIG MATCH!

MUH DADDY...

NAH, HE CAN'T BE HERE.

HE'S ALWAYS BEEN TOO BUSY. HE NEVER TOOK ME HIKING OR PLAYED BASEBALL WITH ME...

ATHLETES! TO THE STARTING LINE!
THEY'RE READY TO GO!
START
THIS BATTLE OULD CHANGE THE COURSE OF THE UPERHUMAN OLYMPICS!
YEEK!
WHAT? IT'S BACK TO A GIRL AGAIN?
A NEW HUMAN SACRIFICE IS PLACED IN THE EVIL MASK'S MOUTH!
HEADS DOWN!
WHATEVER HAPPENS, ONLY ONE OF THESE THREE WILL ADVANCE TO THE NEXT EVENT!
EADY ... GET ET...

GOAL
PAK
BANG
GO!
DASH
THE SIGNAL GUN HAS FIRED FOR A RACE THAT WILL SURELY GO DOWN IN SUPERHUMAN OLYMPICS HISTORY!
GREECE'S BARONUS, IN THE SECOND LANE, GETS A LATE START!
HEH HEH... I FELL BACK ON PURPOSE!

SAND WALL!
SHUK
WAK
BARONUS KICKS SAND INTO THE LANES TO EACH SIDE!
ZZ
WHOA!
WMM
OH! THE GROUND BARONUS KICKED...
THE SURFACE OF THE EARTH RISES AND MOVES FORWARD LIKE A LIVING CREATURE!
K
WHAT THE--
...RISES IN FRONT OF TERRY KENYON AND JAEGER!
WMMM

D

HEH HEH! IT WORKED PERFECTLY!

AK

BARONUS SHOWS OFF HIS MOVES AND QUICKLY TAKES THE LEAD!

THUK

A GIANT WALL OF SAND BLOCKS THEIR PATHS!

ARGH!

THUK

DAK

TERRY KENYON AND JAEGER GET UP AND CHASE BARONUS!

HEH HEH! PESTS!

DAK

SHP

THAT VILL-AIN!

HE AIN'T GETTIN' AWAY WITH THIS!

SHUF

BARONUS NOTICES AND QUICKLY JUMPS...

BAM

...AIMING A STRADDLE KICK AT TERRY KENYON AND JAEGER!

BUT BOTH MEN SKILLFULLY EVADE IT!

DAK

WHAT? MY PERFECT PLAN!

SHF

BAM

NOT GOOD ENOUGH, BARON-US!
YOUR WILL TO WIN IS NOTHING NEXT TO OURS!
WHAK
IN AN AMAZING CONVERGENCE, KENYON AND JAEGER LAND MATCHING ROLLING SOBUTS TO BARONUS'S FACE!
KAFF...
SHUP
OH! BARONUS IS DOWN FOR THE COUNT!

WITH BARONUS OUT OF THE RACE, THIS DECISIVE BATTLE HAS COME DOWN TO...
DAK

...KENYON AND JAEGER!
TERRY! TERRY!
JAEGER! JAEGER!

...!?
...

WAAH!
FWASH
!

I-I'M THE ONLY ONE WHO SEES 'EM!

DAK

FOR THE TERRY FAMILY, WINNING THE SUPERHUMAN OLYMPICS...
...IS AN AMBITION SPANNING 38 YEARS!
DAK

KENYON AND JAEGER ARE NECK TO NECK!

JAEGER, TAKE CARE OF THE GIRL FOR ME!

KENYON!

DAK

EEEK!

GRAB

BAH

WHAT'S GOING ON? WITH THE GOAL ONLY SECONDS AWAY...
...TERRY KENYON SUDDENLY VEERS OFF COURSE TOWARD THE OCEAN!
AL
OH! GERMANY'S JAEGER WINS THIS HISTORIC RACE TO ADVANCE TO THE FOURTH EVENT!
WA
A
TERRY KEN-YON...
THE SUPERHUMAN OLYMPIC DREAM HAS ONCE AGAIN CRUMBLED FOR THE TERRY FAMILY!
JAEGER

SPLISH
SPLISH

TERRY...
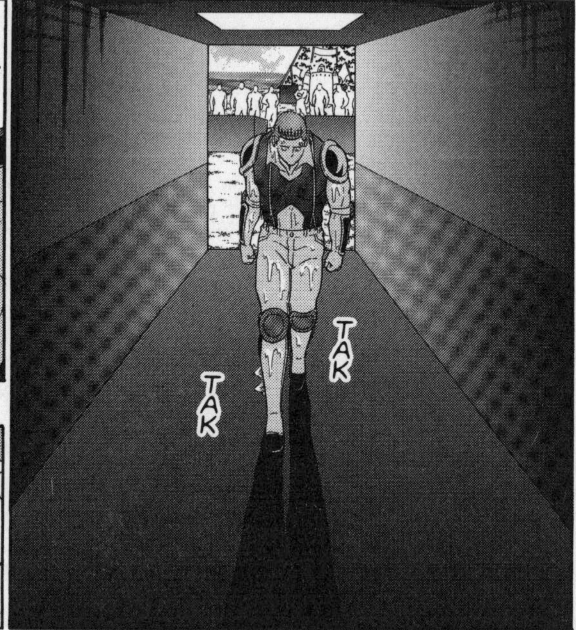
TAK
TAK

SOME DEFEATS...
...ARE MORE HONORABLE THAN ALL THE WORLD'S VICTORIES.

I'M PROUD OF YA, SON!
DAD ...

CHAPTER 133: WHEEZING FOR A PARTNER

THIS IS THE 15-KILOMETER TOKYO BAY AQUA-LINE, WHICH CONNECTS THE CITIES OF KAWASAKI AND KISARAZU.

ON THE AQUA-LINE, WHERE THE TUNNEL AND BRIDGE MEET, IS "SEA FIREFLY," A UNIQUE AMUSEMENT PARK ON THE SEA!

THE 65 SUPERHUMANS WHO PASSED THE THIRD EVENT ARE ALREADY GATHERED ON THE DECK!

...RHUMAN OLYMPICS RESURRECTION

MMF...YOU CAN SEE ALL THE WAY TO MT. FUJI TODAY!

READ
THIS
WAY

EVEN THE CHAIRMAN IS SLACKING OFF!

AND NOW A WORD FROM THE SUPER-HUMAN OLYMPICS CHAIRMAN...
...MR. IKEMEN MCMADD!

AHEM.

KOFF
SHF

TODAY IS THE FINAL EVENT...
...OF THE QUALIFYING ROUND OF THE SUPERHUMAN OLYMPICS!

BUT IT'S NO USE SHOVING HARSH REALITY IN YOUR FACES.

BEFORE WE START THE FINAL EVENT, I'D LIKE ALL OF YOU TO DO SOMETHING.

HERE IN THE STANDS OF THE SEA FIREFLY PARK...

...SEVERAL THOUSAND PEOPLE HAVE GATHERED TO WATCH THE SUPERHUMAN OLYMPICS.

READ THIS WAY

COME ON! IT'S NICE OF THE COMMITTEE TO TREAT US...

...TO A LITTLE DOWNTIME WITH THE FANS.

HMM...

DEE DEE DEE...

WHO SHOULD I PICK?

WAA

EEE! PICK ME, KEVIN MASK!

WAAA

PICK *ME*, JAEGER!

RICARDO, PICK *ME*!

I'M YOUR BIGGEST FAN, COMRADE TURBINSKI!

HEY THERE.

HEY!

WHOA! SHE'S TOTALLY MY TYPE!

PLEASE BE MY PARTNER!

ZOOM

SHA...

READ THIS WAY

I WANT YOU, BINGO-MAN!
SORRY, MAN-TARO.
BINGO
NO WAY! YOU'RE CHOOSING THIS FREAK OVER ME?

ALL RIGHT! YOU, THEN!

I'VE ALREADY SETTLED ON HIM!
NOT AGAIN!
SHA

HOW ABOUT YOU?
SWEET!

YOU THERE!

I'LL TAKE YOU!
WHEE!!

SUPERHUMANS AND SPECTATORS ARE PAIRING OFF ON THE FIREFLY DECK!
NO...
OH, BOY!
C'MON!
YOU!

YES!

ALL RIGHT. LORD FLASH, I'LL PAIR WITH YOU!

TUP
OH! KEVIN MASK CHOOSES A MYSTER-IOUS...
...COSTUMED MAN FROM THE STANDS!

HEY! YOU GOT A PARTNER ALREADY, EZO MAN?
NO!
IS KEVIN MASK GAY?
WITH ALL THESE GIRLS TO CHOOSE FROM, HE GOES FOR SOME DUDE?

ARGH... I'M WASTING TIME!
AHA
I'D BETTER PARTNER UP WITH SOMEBODY, QUICK!
YUP! MANTARO, LET ME INTRODUCE YOU TO MY FATHER.
I'M FROM KAGOSHIMA.
WHOA... HIS MASK'S IN THE SHAPE OF KAGOSHIMA!
北海道

JAEGER! OVER HERE! PICK ME!
NO, IGNORE THAT SKANK! PICK ME!
JAEGER!
JAEGER!
EEK! JAEGER!

HUH?
M-ME?

FRAU-
LEIN...
...WILL
YOU
BE MY
PARTNER?

SURE,
IF
YOU'RE
OKAY
WITH IT.

DANKE.
HERE,
TAKE MY
HAND!
THANKS.
GOOD LUCK
BOO!

ROXANNE...

OH, ROX-ANNE!

ROX-ANNE!

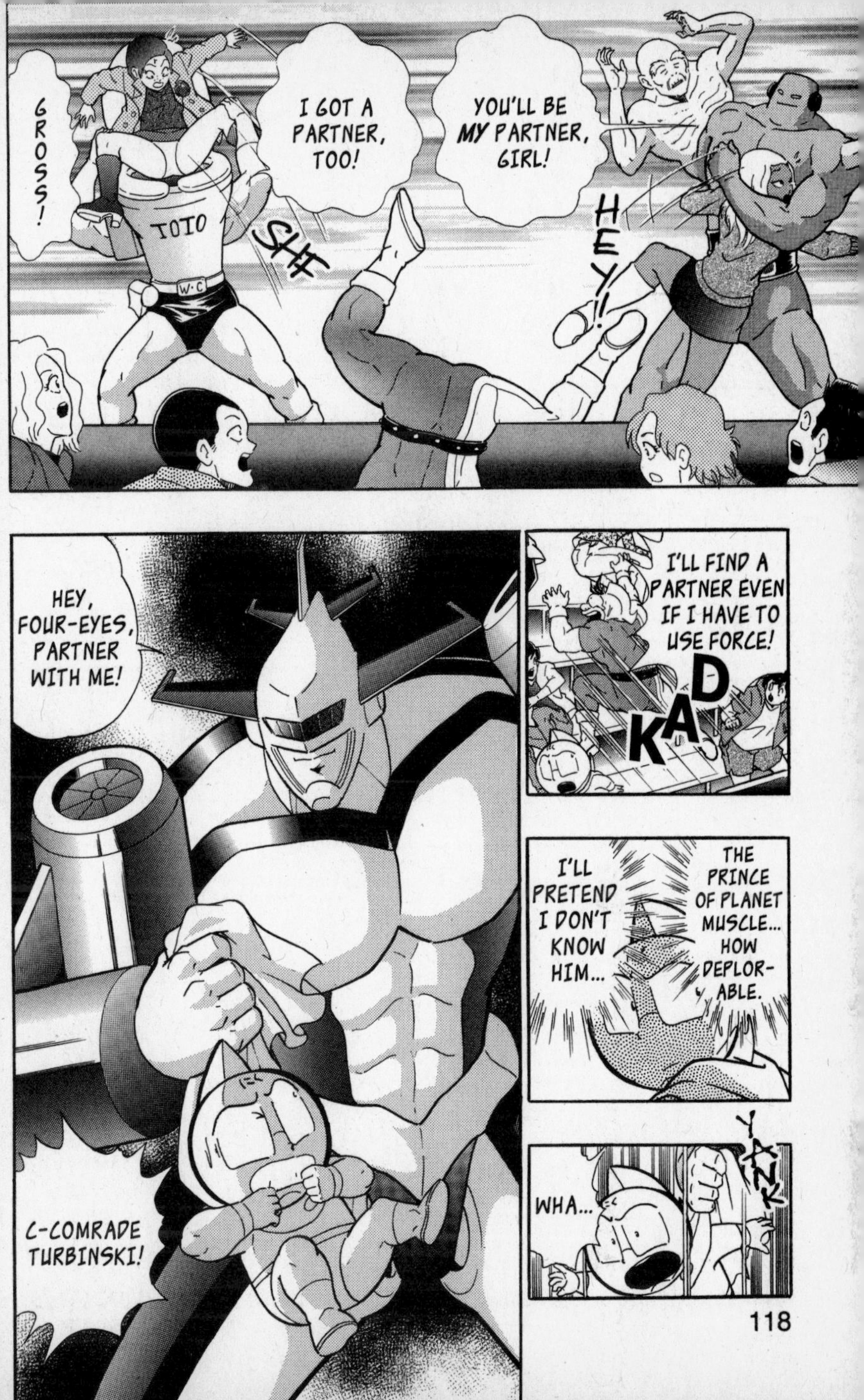

YOU'LL BE *MY* PARTNER, GIRL!
HEY!!
I GOT A PARTNER, TOO!
SH
GROSS!

HEY, FOUR-EYES, PARTNER WITH ME!
C-COMRADE TURBINSKI!

I'M KID MUSCLE'S MANAGER!
WHY SHOULD I PAIR WITH YOU?
GRAB
JUST SHUT UP AND BE MY PARTNER!
SQUICK
UGH... UGH...

HEY! YOU'RE THE BALD DUDE...

...I SAVED IN THE LAST ROUND!

...YA WANT *ME* AS YOUR PARTNER?

HUH?

MY NAME'S YONEO SASAKI.

NOT ONLY DID YA SAVE ME THEN...

...NOW YOU'RE PICKIN' ME AS YOUR PARTNER!

...

GRAB

OH, NO!

HE'S LOVIN' IT!

LOOKS LIKE YOU EACH FOUND A PARTNER TO YOUR LIKING.

CHOOSING A PARTNER WAS PREPARATION FOR THE FINAL COMPETITION.
WHAT ARE YOU TALKING ABOUT, MANTARO?
HEY, CHAIRMAN! THAT'S ENOUGH GETTING-TO-KNOW-YOU TIME!
LET'S DITCH THE FANS AND MOVE ON!
THIS WASN'T JUST FOR FUN?
WHAT?

READ THIS WAY

DO YOU ALL REMEMBER THE ITEM WE GAVE YOU WHEN YOU ENTERED THE PARK?

ITEM?

YOU WILL BIND EACH OTHER'S ANKLES...

...WITH THAT LEATHER BELT!

HA

AND NOW FOR THE FINAL COMPE-TITION...

...IN THE QUALIFYING ROUND OF THE SUPER-HUMAN OLYMPICS...

WHEEZY WHEEZY THREE-LEGGED RACE!
"WHEEZY WHEEZY THREE-LEGGED RACE!"
POW
HUH?

CHAPTER 134: OBSTACLES IN THE PATH

WHEEZY WHEEZY THREE-LEGGED RACE!

THE FINAL COMPETITION ANNOUNCED BY CHAIRMAN IKEMEN IS A THREE-LEGGED RACE!

IT'D BE FASTER IF WE RAN ALONE!
YEAH!
JUST LET US RUN!
BAM
NOW, NOW. WHAT KIND OF CHALLENGE...
...WOULD THAT BE?

IF I'D KNOWN *THAT*, I WOULD'VE PICKED A BUFF DUDE INSTEAD OF CHASING HOTTIES!
YOU AND ME BOTH...
EW! I HATE RUNNING!
RUN? IN *THESE* SHOES?

HEY, IF YOU WANT A GUY, YOU CAN SWITCH WITH ME!
YEAH?
ER...
N-NO THANKS!

THE COURSE WILL START HERE, AT UMI-HOTARU, AND MOVE TOWARD KAWASAKI.
YOU'LL FOLLOW THE BAYSHORE ROUTE...
...PAST HANEDA AIRPORT, ACROSS THE RAINBOW BRIDGE, AND FINISHING AT ODAIBA'S KAIHIN PARIK!
ODAIBA KEIHIN PARK
RAINBOW BRIDGE
METROPOLITAN EXPRESSWAY
BAYSHORE ROUTE
風神

ORDINARILY, UMI-HOTARU IS CONNECTED TO KAWASAKI...

...BY A TUNNEL BENEATH TOKYO BAY.

BUT FOR THE SUPER-HUMAN OLYMPICS...

...WE'VE PREPARED A SPECIAL THREE-LEGGED RACE-TRACK!

KLIK

GRRRM

FSSSH

WHOA! WHAT'S GOING ON?

FSHHHH

LOOK! SOME-THING'S RISING OUT OF THE SEA!

IT'S A ROAD!
A ROAD ACROSS THE OCEAN!
FSSSH
FOLLOW THE THREE-LEGGED RACETRACK...
...ALL THE WAY TO KAIHIN PARK!

AW, MAN!

WOW! WE'LL BE TOGETHER FOREVER!

SIT STILL, FOUR-EYES!

GUESS YOU REGRET PICKING ME...

...HUH, JAEGER?

NEIN.

I DIDN'T CHOOSE YOU FOR INDECENT REASONS.

OUT OF EVERYONE IN THE STANDS...

...I SAW THE GREATEST STRENGTH IN YOUR EYES.

...

WHAT'S GOING ON HERE?
HE'S TALKING DIRTY TO YOU, ISN'T HE?
FWOK
WHY DON'T YOU GO CUDDLE WITH YOUR NEW *BOY-FRIEND?*
GRP
OKAY, IT'S DONE!
LEAVE IT TO ME, JAEGER. I MIGHT NOT LOOK IT, BUT I'M PRETTY ATHLETIC!
I'M COUNTING ON YOU!
THE LEATHER BELTS OF THE 65 SUPERHUMANS AND THEIR PARTNERS HAVE BEEN SECURED. THEY ARE NOW READY FOR WAR!

GO!!
AT THE CHAIRMAN'S SIGNAL, 65 MIXED PAIRS BEGIN THE THREE-LEGGED RACE...
...TOWARD KAIHIN PARK!
DAK
DAK
DAK
HEH HEH HEH... DO THEY THINK THIS IS AN ORDINARY RACE?
HEH HEH...
THEY DON'T KNOW THE HELL THAT AWAITS THEM...
HEH HEH...

TMP
TMP
RIGHT! LEFT!
LEFT! RIGHT!
NO, MR. SASAKI! IT'S RIGHT, LEFT, RIGHT, LEFT!
TMP
WHAT? NOT LEFT, RIGHT?
WAAAH!
AIEEE!
WAK!
GYAA!
TMP
TMP
TMP
OWW...
TMP
UGH!

A WALL! A GIANT WALL!
NO, IT'S NOT A WALL!
THE ROAD HAS BEEN LIFTED LIKE A DRAW-BRIDGE!
WUP WUP
WUP WUP
LADIES AND GENTLEMEN! I FORGOT TO MENTION THAT THERE ARE OBSTACLES ALONG THE THREE-LEGGED RACECOURSE!
YOU MUST CLEAR THEM ALL TO REACH THE GOAL!

ME AND MAD SKELETON ARE GONNA BE THE FIRST PAIR IN ODAIBA!

YAHOO!

TAK TAK TAK

TAK

TAK

THE MAD SKELETON PAIR JUMPS OUT OF THE CROWD TO CHALLENGE THE WALL!

?

WHOA!

TAK

I-I CAN'T MOVE MY LEGS...

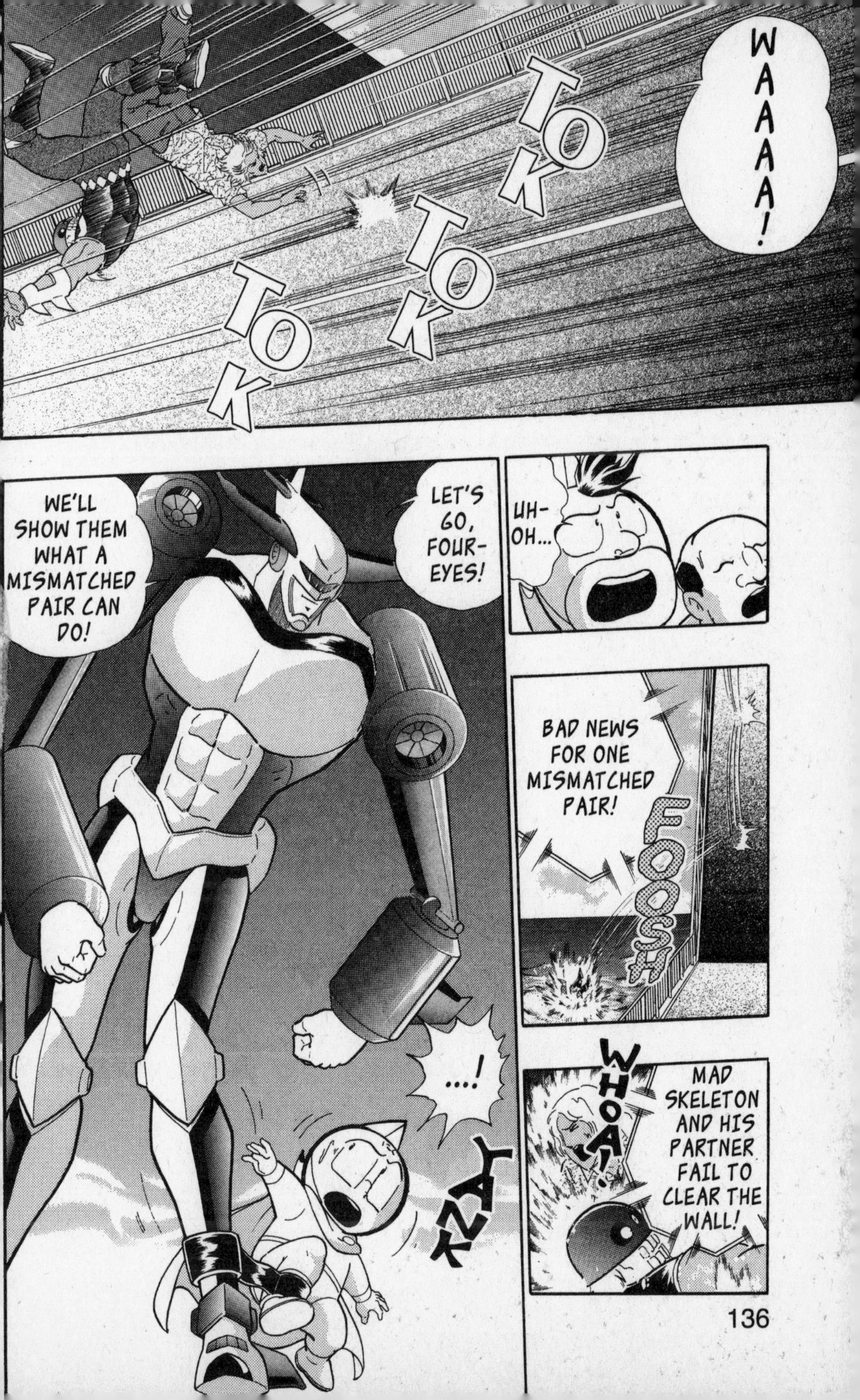

LET'S GO, FOUR-EYES!

WE'LL SHOW THEM WHAT A MISMATCHED PAIR CAN DO!

...!

TZAY

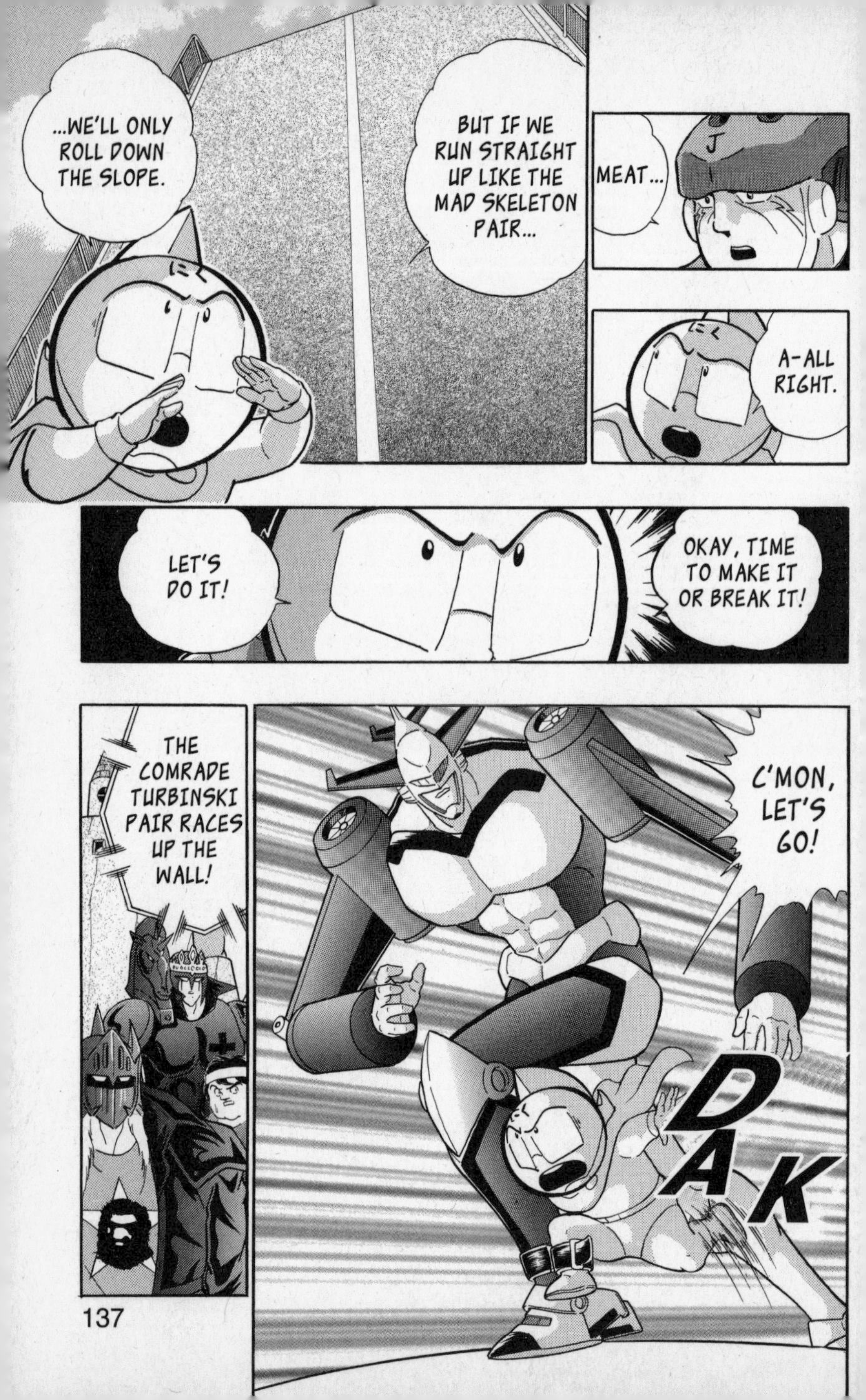

...WE'LL ONLY ROLL DOWN THE SLOPE.

BUT IF WE RUN STRAIGHT UP LIKE THE MAD SKELETON PAIR...

MEAT...

A-ALL RIGHT.

LET'S DO IT!

OKAY, TIME TO MAKE IT OR BREAK IT!

THE COMRADE TURBINSKI PAIR RACES UP THE WALL!

C'MON, LET'S GO!

DAK

Tak

Tak

Tak

Tak

INSTEAD OF RUNNING STRAIGHT UP, THEY RUN DIAGONALLY!

BUT MEAT'S TOO MUCH OF A BURDEN.

W-WE'RE ALMOST THERE...

wobble

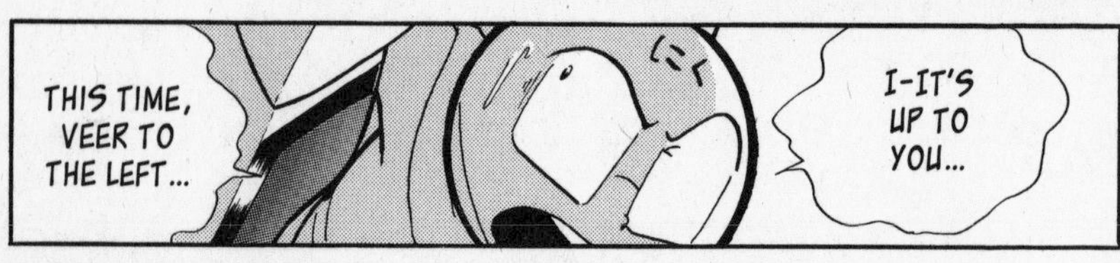

ALL RIGHT!

DAK

COMRADE TURBINSKI TAKES THE LEAD, RUNNING DIAGONALLY TO THE LEFT!

WITH THIS BRILLIANT ZIG-ZAG METHOD, THE COMRADE TURBINSKI PAIR...
TUP
...REACHES THE TOP OF THE WALL...
...TO TAKE THE LEAD!
TAK TAK
TAK TAK
MY CHOICE WAS CORR-ECT.
TAK
?
HFF
HFF
YOU HAPPEN TO BE KID MUSCLE'S ADVISOR.
BUT YOU'RE WILLING TO SHARE YOUR GENIUS...
...WITH ANYONE FROM THE JUSTICE FEDERATION!

THAT MOVE WAS ONLY POSSIBLE WITH MEAT'S TACTICAL BRILLIANCE ...

SLAP SLAP

...AND COMRADE TURBINSKI'S POWER.

!

WE'LL TACKLE IT HEAD-ON.

THERE'S NO STOPPING IN THE MIDDLE, ROXANNE, SO KEEP UP!

OKAY!

DAK

LET'S GO!

GIRL POWER!

I DON'T BELIEVE IT!

TAK TAK TAK

TAK

THE JAEGER PAIR RUNS STRAIGHT UP THE WALL!

JAEGER IS IMPRESSIVE, BUT HIS PARTNER IS EVEN MORE AMAZING!
TAK
TAK TAK
THEY'RE ALMOST AT THE TOP!
Hff
WFF
WOK
AHH!

FOOSH
RED RAIN OF PAIN!!
THE JAEGER PAIR JUST BARELY CLEARS THE TOP!
WAK

FR... FRAULEIN ...
C'MON! LET'S GO!

ALL RIGHT!
dak
THE JAEGER PAIR HEADS TOWARD ODAIBA IN SECOND PLACE!

WE CAN'T JUST STAND AROUND!

DAKKA

MEAN-WHILE ...
TUP TUP TUP
WAIT UP!!

CHAPTER 135:

SECRETS OF THE CHOSEN ONES

TAK TAK TAK TAK TAK

MOST OF THE PAIRS HAVE TO ATTEMPTED TO CLEAR THE FIRST OBSTACLE...

TAK TAK

...AND ONLY A FEW REMAIN!

WE'RE FINALLY LEARNING TO MATCH OUR STRIDES!
1!
2!
IT'S TOO LATE! WE'RE TOO FAR BEHIND!
TAK TAK TAK

ARRGH!
WAK!
YIKES...

WHAT HAPPENED TO THE ROAD?
UGH...
IT'S LITTERED WITH THE BODIES OF EVERYONE WHO DIDN'T CLEAR THE SLOPE!
Beef

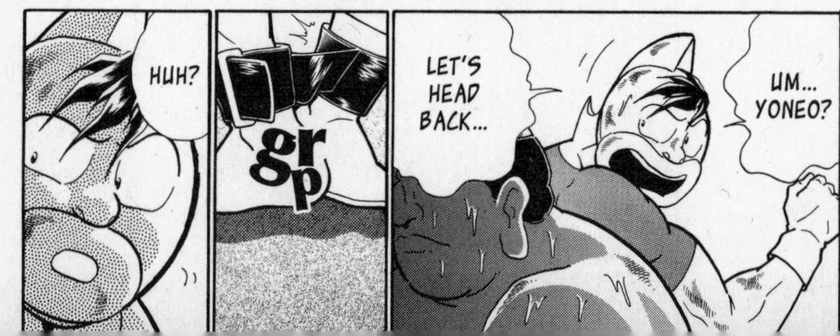
UM... YONEO?
LET'S HEAD BACK...
grp
HUH?

YO-
NEO?
I WAS CHOSEN AS THE PARTNER OF KID MUSCLE...
...THE BEARER OF THE FIRE.

I'LL DO EVERYTHING IN MY POWER TO HELP YOU FINISH THIS RACE...
...AND ADVANCE TO THE SUPERHUMAN OLYMPICS FINALS!

I ONLY CHOSE HIM...
...BY ACCIDENT.

ER... ACTUALLY, MY *LIFE* IS MORE IMPORT-ANT...
...THAN SOME STUPID CONTEST, SO LET'S GO BACK!

READY?
VOOP
STOP IT, YONEO! YOU WEIGH A TON!
YOU CAN'T RUN UP THIS SLOPE!

THE KID MUSCLE PAIR GOES FOR THE WALL!
THEY RUN TOWARD IT AT TREMENDOUS SPEED!
Tak Tak
Tak
ALL RIGHT! JUMP!
HUH? JUMP?
OH! THESE TWO AREN'T RUNNING UP THE WALL!
THEY'RE TRYING TO JUMP **OVER** IT!

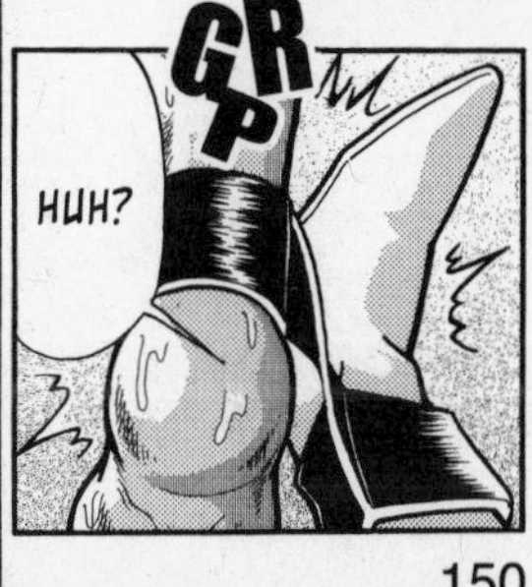

GLORP

WAIT! THE BODY OF KID MUSCLE'S PARTNER STICKS TO THE SLOPE, PREVENTING THEM FROM FALLING!

WH-WHAT THE...

OOG...
SPLORP!...
HEH... I GUESS MY SWEAT *IS* PRETTY STICKY.
IT'S HOLDING ME TO THE SLOPE LIKE A SUCTION CUP!

GLORP
GLORP
LIKE A GIANT SLUG, KID MUSCLE'S PARTNER SLITHERS UP...
...USING THE STICKINESS OF HIS SWEAT!
ALL RIGHT, KID MUS-CLE!
GLORP
HOLD ON TIGHT!
GLORP

THIS IS A TRULY HORRIFIC IMAGE! I CAN'T BELIEVE A HUMAN CAN DO THIS!

GLORP

ALL RIGHT! GO YONEO! WE'RE ALMOST THERE!

GLOP

WE... WE MADE IT...

GLOM

GOOD JOB!

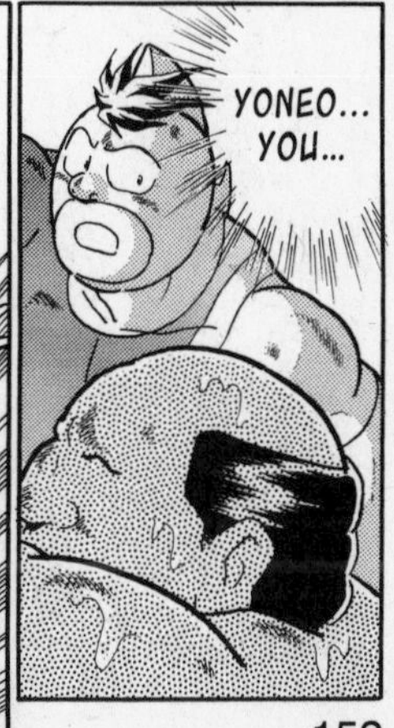

HUH?

MEANWHILE, THE PAIRS AT THE HEAD OF THE RACE ENTER THE METROPOLITAN EXPRESSWAY!

TAK

TAK

LOOK!

THE COMRADE TURBINSKI PAIR HAD AN EASY LEAD FOR A WHILE, BUT NOW THE RUNNERS ARE IN A PACK!

TAK

TAK

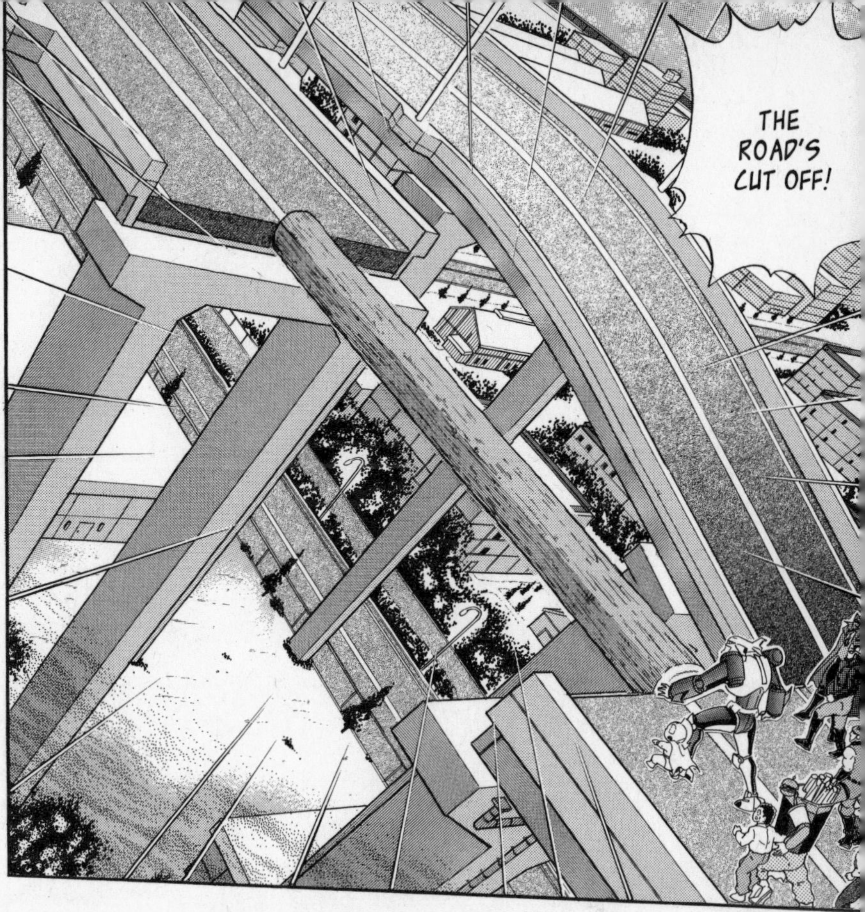

THE ROAD'S CUT OFF!

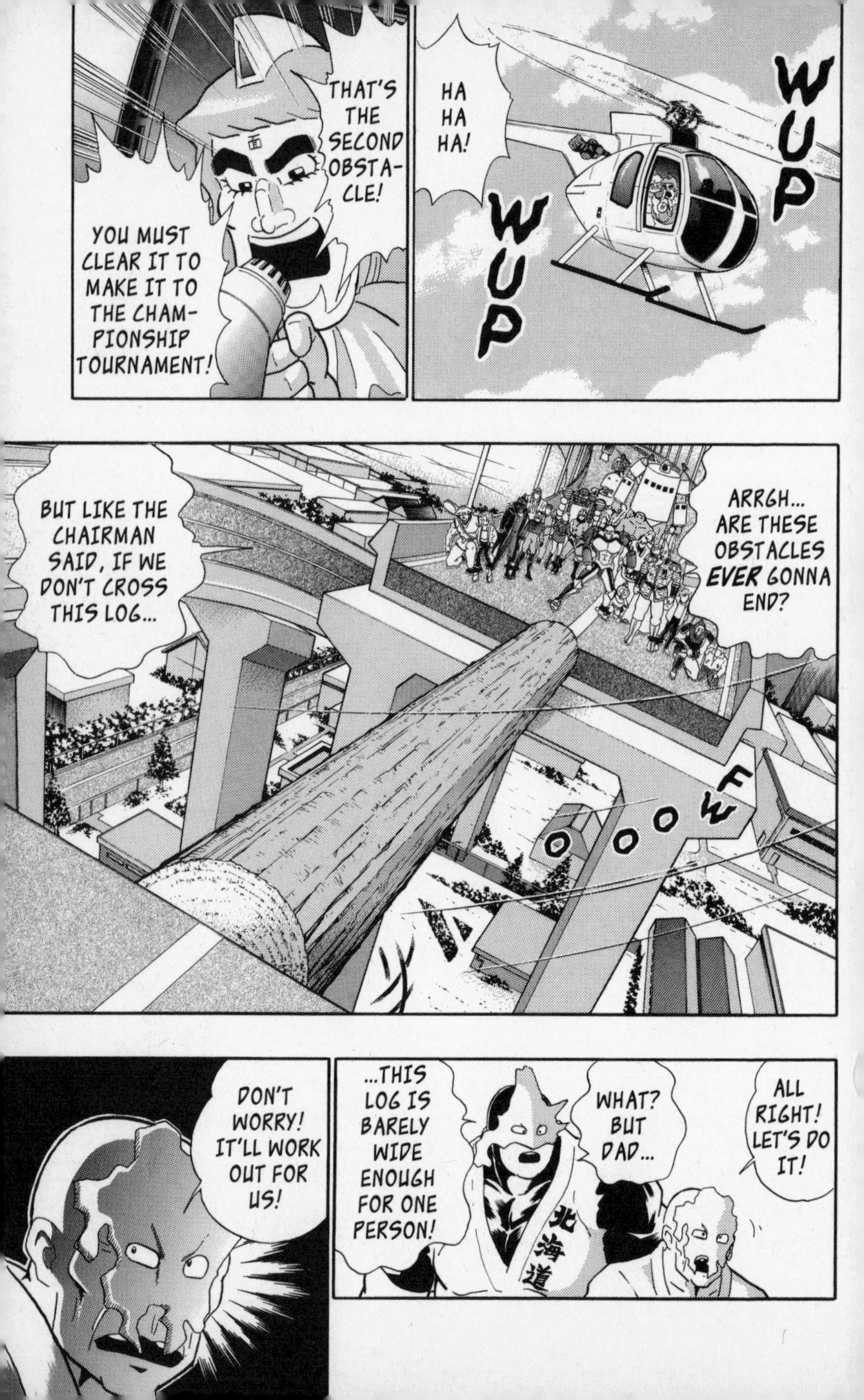

ARRGH... ARE THESE OBSTACLES *EVER* GONNA END?

BUT LIKE THE CHAIRMAN SAID, IF WE DON'T CROSS THIS LOG...

FWOOOO

SLOWLY... SLOWLY...

Y-YEAH...

EASY, DAD!

WE'LL CROSS IT SIDEWAYS!

EZO MAN AND HIS FATHER INCH ALONG THE LOG...

...SIDEWAYS!

OH! THE LOG IS NOT SECURE!
YIPE! THE LOG'S ROLL-ING!
IT'S DESIGNED TO ROLL IF YOU'RE OFF-BALANCE!
GO RO
GO RO
GO RO
THE OLYMPIC COMMIT-TEE WOULDN'T GO *THAT* EASY ON US.
GO RO..
EZO MAN!
WAAA!
D-DAD!
GRP
WAP
THE EZO MAN PAIR FALLS STRAIGHT DOWN!!

BUT AT THE END OF THE FALL...
...
BOING
...THE PAIR IS SAVED BY A SAFETY NET!

!

FORGIVE ME, SON. I MADE A TERRIBLE MISTAKE.

IT'S ALL RIGHT. LIKE THE SHORT SPRING OF HOKKAIDO...
...THE SPRINGTIME OF THE SUPERHUMAN OLYMPICS HAS ENDED.
SON...

READ THIS WAY

ONLY SUPERHUMANS WITH AN INSTINCT FOR HANDLING SURPRISES...

...WILL MAKE IT THROUGH TO THE FINALS!

DAK

KEVIN ...

KEVIN MASK AND HIS PARTNER TRY THEIR LUCK!

BUT THEY QUICKLY LOSE THEIR BALANCE!

GORO

KEVIN MASK! **SPIRAL RUNNING!**

RIGHT!

INSTEAD OF BALANCING ON THE LOG, THE KEVIN MASK PAIR...
TAK
TAK
TAK
TAK
TAK
...TURNS TO THE ROTATION OF THE LOG AND RUNS IN A SPIRAL MOTION!

DAK

TAK

TAK

BY COMBINING THEIR BRAINS AND ATHLETIC PROWESS...

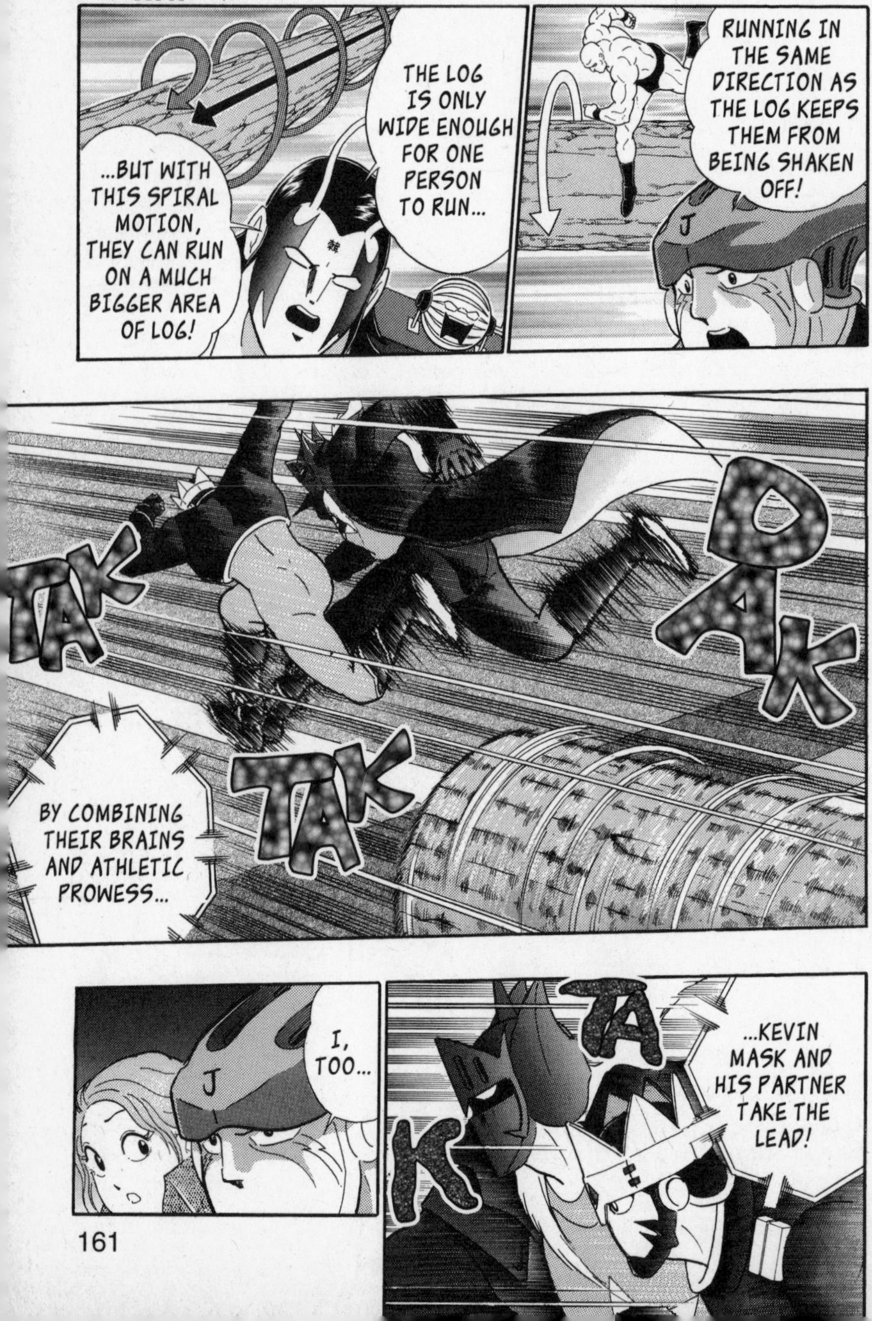

TOK

THE JAEGER PAIR LANDS ON THE LOG FACING IN OPPOSITE DIRECTIONS!

YOOP

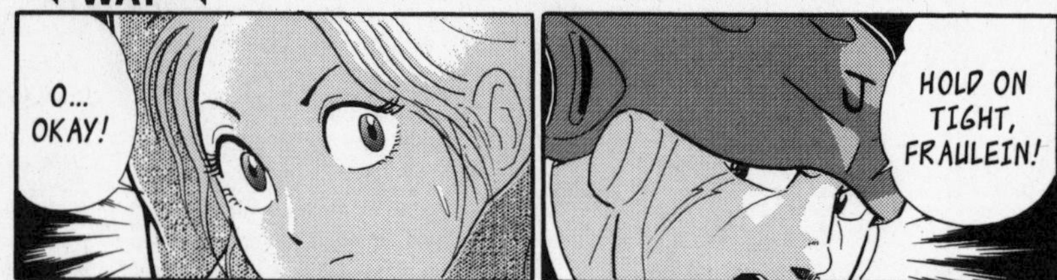

HI-YAH!

YEEK!

VWM
VWM
WHOA...
VWM

CHAPTER 136:
THREE-LEGGED RACE: THE FINAL BATTLE

SUPERHUMANS APPEARING IN CHAPTERS 133, 135, AND 136 WERE BASED ON THE IDEAS FROM THE FOLLOWING READERS:

KAZ-MARU (AGE 22)
HIDEKAZU KURUSU (AGE 27)
FUMIHIKO ISHIZAWA (AGE 25)
NARU MATSUYAMA (AGE 28)
RICHARD (AGE 23)
YOSHIKI SUZUKI (AGE 17)
SHOUJI ICHIKAWA (AGE 20)
AKIRA HIRAISHI (AGE 10)
TARO IKEDA (AGE 26)
TETSUYA HARADA (AGE 19)
TESTUYA KONDO (AGE 26)
TAKAYUKI SASAKI (AGE 26)
KOUTOKU HATA (AGE 27)
TAISUKE MIZOROGI (AGE 21)
MASAAKI IIZUKA (AGE 24)
KAZUKI KAGAMI (AGE 20)
ATSUSHI SHIMOKAWA (AGE16)
TAKESHI YAGI (AGE 31)
RIKITO HAMADA (AGE 22)

THEY REACH THE OTHER SIDE OF THE GAP!

VWM

FLP

W-WE MADE IT?

REALLY?

ROXANNE... JUST AS I THOUGHT, YOU'RE A BRAVE WOMAN.

PLEASE SUPPORT ME FOR A LITTLE LONGER.

HEY! WE CAN DO IT, TOO!

GAK

GAK

ONE PAIR AFTER ANOTHER TACKLED THE LOG BRIDGE.

EACH SUPERHUMAN TOOK ADVANTAGE OF HIS UNIQUE SKILLS AND CAME UP WITH A CREATIVE WAY TO CROSS.

VOOM

BUT FOR EVERY TEAM THAT SUCCEEDED, MANY FAILED.
THUD
FOOM

WHILE THE LEADERS OF THE RACE MOVE ON...
TAK
TAK
TAK
...THE REST COME CHARGING TOWARD THE LOG BRIDGE!

THESE PAIRS ARE TRAILING IN THE RACE...
...BUT IF THEY CAN CROSS THE LOG BRIDGE, THEY STILL HAVE A CHANCE!
TAK
TAK

WUP
ARRGH! HOW COULD MANTARO MAKE IT THIS FAR?
WUP

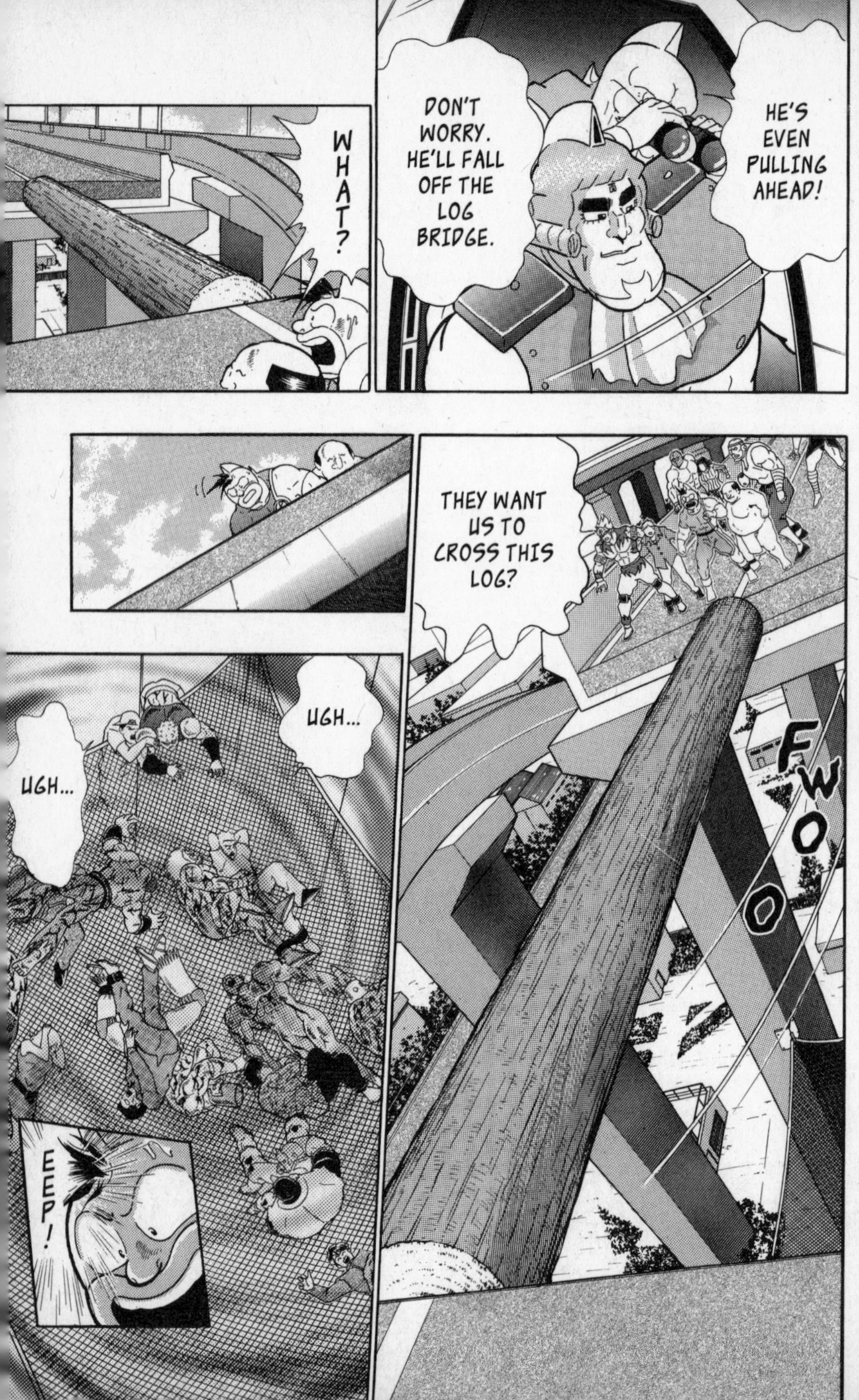
HE'S EVEN PULLING AHEAD!
DON'T WORRY. HE'LL FALL OFF THE LOG BRIDGE.
WHAT?
THEY WANT US TO CROSS THIS LOG?
FWOOO
UGH...
UGH...
EEEP!

HEH HEH... NO PROBLEM!
SLAP
SLAP
I'LL TURN THAT LOG INTO A CORK TO PLUG MY FARTS!
SUCH CONFI-DENCE!

HURRY UP, MAN-TARO!
C'MON, YONEO!

YOU MUST HAVE ANOTHER SECRET STRATEGY...
...LIKE YOUR STICKY SWEAT!

SH-ING!
ER... I THINK I'M ALL SWEATED OUT.
FUMP

WUP
WHAT ARE THEY WAITING FOR?
WUP
IF THOSE TWO FOOLS DON'T FALL SOON...
OH, NO!
AND I'M REALLY SCARED OF HEIGHTS...
PSS

FORCE HIM ACROSS, MANTARO!
OOF
WHOA!
DON'T JUST STAND THERE, YOU BALD LITTLE FREAK!
WUP
WUP
GRRR
SIR, BE CAREFUL!

FWE
LOOK! THE HELI-COPTER'S FALLING!
WAAAA!
EEEE
WAAAA!
EEEEK!
HUH?
VWEEEE
IT'S TOO LATE!
DAK
VWEEEE
NOOOO!
IT'S GONNA CRASH!

...!
VWOOM
RUNNING FROM THE CRASHING HELICOPTER, THE KID MUSCLE PAIR JUMPS ONTO THE LOG BRIDGE!
GSSH
KID MUSCLE AND HIS PARTNER...
GATUNK
YIKES!
...BOTH CLUTCH THE LOG WITH THEIR LEGS!

WOOSH
WOOSH
WHOA!
WOOSH
WOOSH
STILL HOLDING ONTO THE LOG WITH THEIR LEGS...
...MANTARO AND HIS PARTNER ADVANCE BY SPINNING AROUND THE LOG!
AUGH!
THE REPAIRS ARE GOING TO COST ME...
HUH?
WHAT?

VWOOSH
VWOOSH
EEK!
VWOOSH
HUH?
WAK!
DSSH!
BOING
UGH...
...

AND KID MUSCLE BRILLIANTLY CLEARS THE SECOND OBSTACLE!
WHAT THE... WE...
WE CROSSED THE LOG BRIDGE!

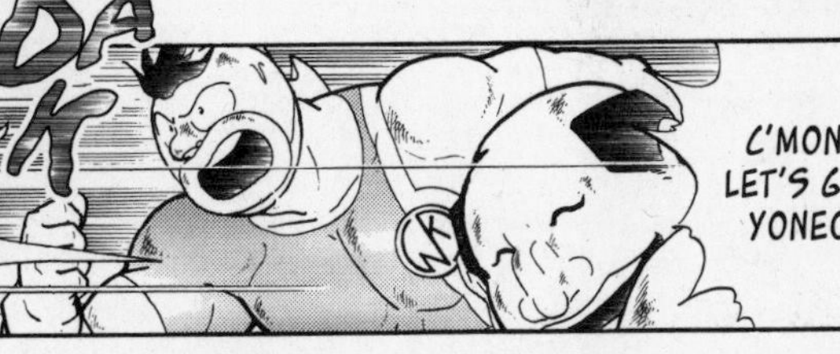

WHY IS IT *ALWAYS* THIS WAY?
ARRGH!

RAINBOW BRIDGE
METROPOLITAN EXPRESSWAY
HANEDA
AS THE RUNNERS PASS HANEDA, THE THREE-LEGGED RACE REACHES ITS CLIMAX!
TAK TAK
THE KEVIN MASK PAIR AND THE JAEGER PAIR HAD THE LEAD, BUT WITH OTHER POWERHOUSES IN THE RACE...
TAK
TAK
...THAT LEAD HAS SHRUNK! AS YOU CAN SEE, SEVERAL RUNNERS ARE NOW VYING FOR FIRST!
TAK TAK
TAK

HA HA
OH! CROATIA'S PURI-KURAN...
HA HA
...SUFFERS INTERFERENCE FROM EFREETMAN AND SNAKE EYE!
KRKKK KRKKK
KRRKKL KRRKKL
EFREET-MAN... SNAKE EYE...
WHAT?

READ THIS WAY

CAN'T SAY NO TO THE GIRLS.
GUESS IT CAN'T HURT.
READY?

SAY CHEESE!
MEMORIES

SMIRK

HURRY, PRINT IT!
HOPE IT COMES OUT GOOD!
THIS IS KINDA EMBARR-ASSING...
EEEEEEEY

TK
THERE IT IS!
PHOTO

WHAT?

MEMORIES
HEY, IT'S ONLY THE SUPERHUMANS! WHERE ARE WE?

HEY! WHERE ARE WE?

EEK! WHERE'D THE SUPER-HUMANS GO?

THEY'RE GONE!

BANG

BANG

BANG

WE'RE TRAPPED INSIDE THE PHOTO!

GET US OUTTA HERE...

WHOA...

BOOM

SMACK DOWN PICTURE!!

UGH!

C'MON, WE SHOULD HURRY!

PRINT CLUB

TA TA TA

THE BATTLE FOR THE LEAD IS HEATING UP!

MOVE!

BAM

YOU'RE IN MY WAY, TWERPS!

GERMANY'S KING CASTLE...

...UNLEASHES A POWERFUL LARIAT ON ENGLAND'S KEVIN MASK AND HIS PARTNER!

GRRK

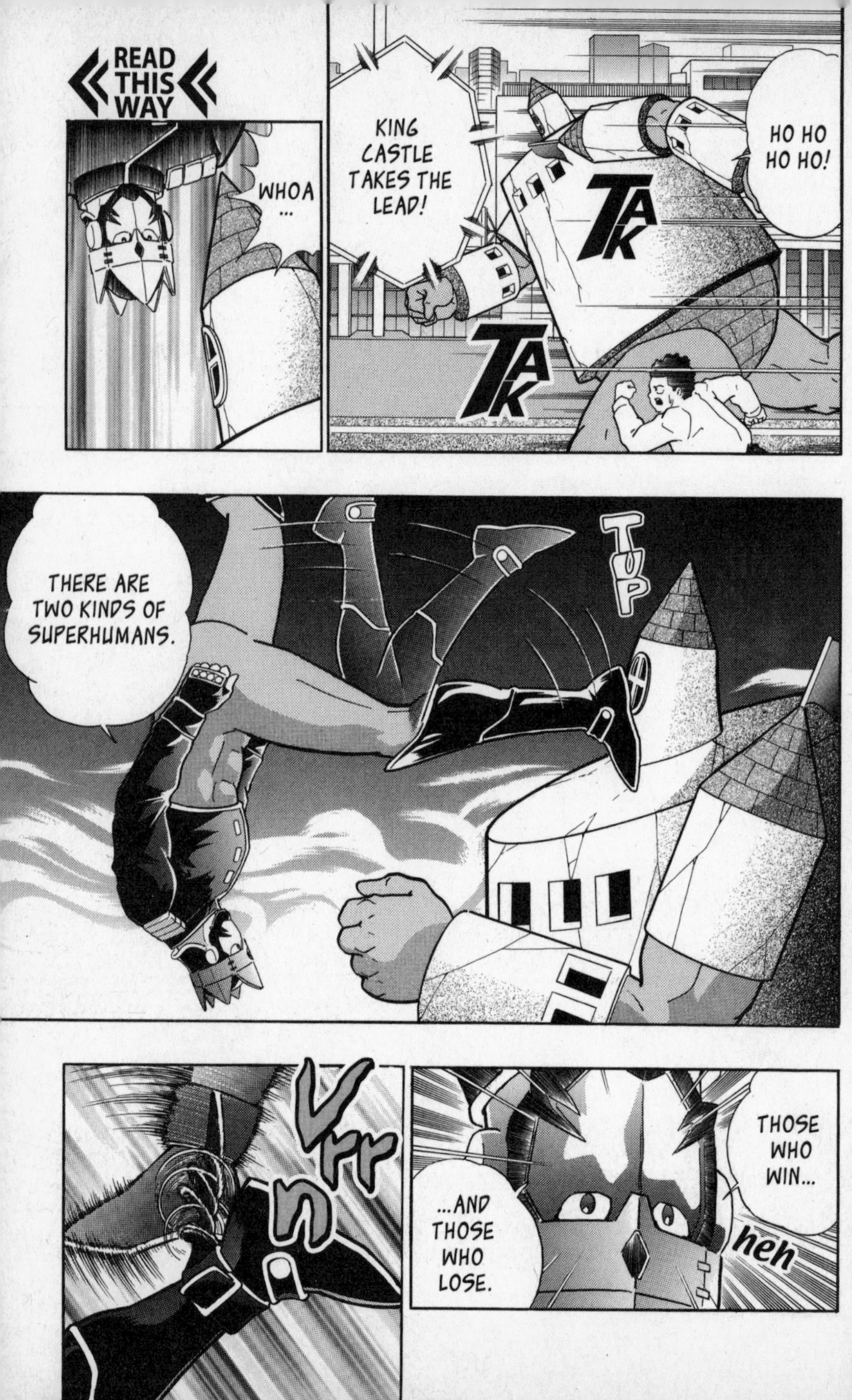

READ THIS WAY

TUP

THERE ARE TWO KINDS OF SUPERHUMANS.

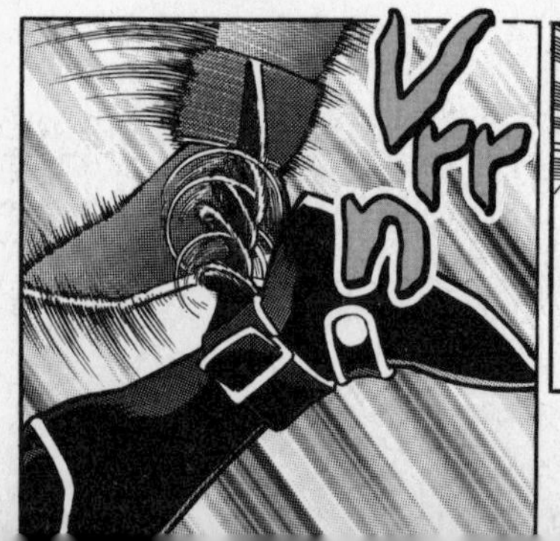

VRRN
YOU, KING CASTLE, ARE ONE OF THE LATTER!
VOOSH

CHAPTER 137:
CAUSE OF DEFEAT

SYNCHRONIZED KICKS FROM KEVIN MASK AND LORD FLASH *CRUSH* KING CASTLE'S HEAD!

KING CASTLE'S HEAD EXPLODES!

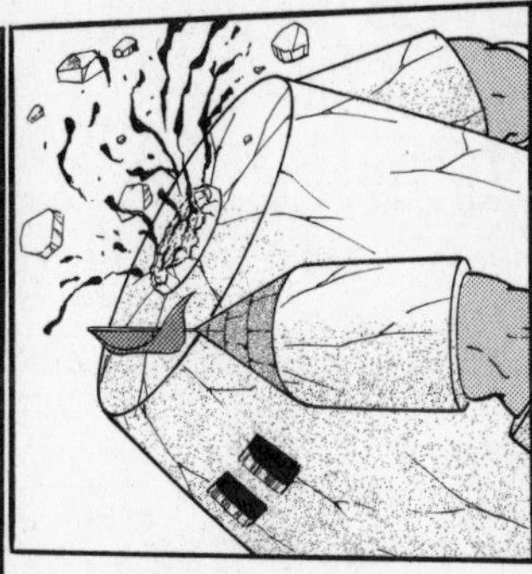

GSSSH
NOOOO!
KING CASTLE IS OUT OF THE RACE!
UGH!
!

IT LOOKS BRUTAL, BUT BLOOD SHED IN THE SUPERHUMAN OLYMPICS...
...IS CONSIDERED AN ACCIDENT OF COMPETITION, NOT A CRIME.

AND KING CASTLE INITIATED THE FIGHT.
THE KEVIN MASK PAIR CANNOT BE CHARGED WITH ANYTHING.
KEVIN MASK MAY BE COMPETING WITH THE JUSTICE FEDER-ATION...
...BUT IT'S CLEAR HE'S AN EX-MEMBER OF THE DMP.
HE HASN'T LOST HIS COLD-HEARTED, MERCILESS NATURE.

READY, LORD FLASH?
YES.
THIS LORD FLASH MUST BE A SUPER-HUMAN.
BUT WHAT KIND?
NOW MOVE!
OH! KEVIN MASK...
...KNOCKS JAEGER OUT OF HIS WAY WITH A JUMPING ELBOW!
UGH!
THUD
JAEGER!
DAK
HE HURRIES BACK TO THE RACE!

READ THIS WAY

COMRADE TURBINSKI! BEHIND YOU!

VOP
NOW MALAYSIA'S MARYU...

...GETS RUSSIA'S COMRADE TURBINSKI IN A FULL NELSON!
HE'S TRYING TO PULL OFF SOME KIND OF MOVE...

HE'S ATTEMPTING A BACK THROW!

THANKS, MEAT! YOU'RE A BIG HELP!

GKK

SHUKK
COMRADE TURBINSKI'S ARMS CHANGE INTO AIRPLANE WINGS!
AIRCRAFT GENETICS!
DEATH-MAMA RIOT!
ZOOP
HE SLIDES OUT OF MARYU'S HOLD!

RAAAH!
DSSH
AS COMRADE TURBINSKI ESCAPES THE HOLD...

AND HISTORY HAS PROVEN THAT ANYONE WHO SURVIVES THIS WAR...
...WILL DEVELOP INTO A GREAT DEFENDER OF PEACE AND JUSTICE.
I WAS BORN A SUPERHUMAN!
I WANT TO KNOW WHAT IT FEELS LIKE TO BE A MUSCLE LEAGUE CHAMPION!
JAEGER ...
I'LL FULFILL THAT DREAM.
GIVE ME A HAND, ROXANNE.
ALL RIGHT!
I'LL DO MY BEST!

HI-
YAH!
THRAK
THE DEAD HEAT AMONG THE LEADS...
VP
C'MON! LET'S GO, JAEGER!
THE JAEGER PAIR GETS BACK TO THE THREE-LEGGED RACE!
TAK
TAK
TAK
UGH!
HUA!
...IS GETTING EVEN **MORE** HEATED!
HI-
YAH!
ARGH!

TAKE THIS!

VOOM

CRSH

AHH!

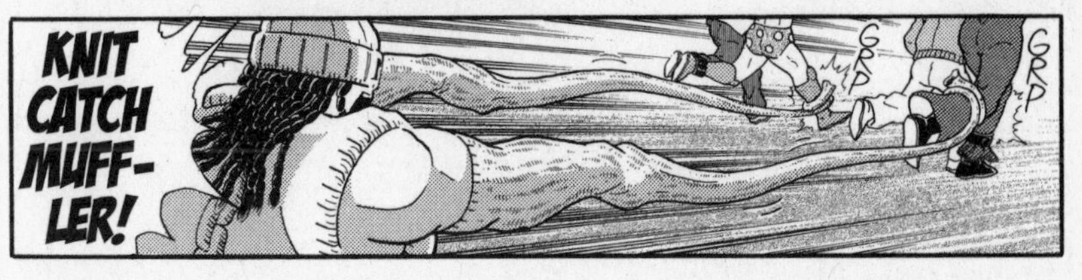

WHOA...

WHOOSH

HEH
GSSSH
KOFF!

WHAT? WE'VE MADE UP SO MUCH GROUND!
WE WERE DEAD LAST, AND NOW WE'RE ALMOST THERE!
I... I DON'T WANNA RUN ANYMORE...

HFF
EVERY-ONE ELSE IS HURTING, TOO...
D-DO YOU THINK YOU'RE THE ONLY ONE SUFFERING?
HFF
B-BUT I'M AT MY LIMIT...

Hff

Hff

Hff

CHECK-MATE!

OH! THE CHECKMATE PAIR, WHICH HAD BEEN IN THE LEAD, SLOWS DOWN!

S-SORRY... YOU SHOULDN'T HAVE PICKED A WIMP LIKE ME...

check mate

NO, SHINYA.

YOU'RE A HUMAN, NOT A SUPER-HUMAN.

YOU WERE INJURED IN A RACE THAT EVEN SUPER-HUMANS FIND DIFFICULT.

BUT LOOK AT ME! I WAS PICKED BY MY FAVORITE WRESTLER, CHECKMATE, AND NOW...

mate

GCH GCH GCH

POP POP POP POP

BELGIUM'S MR. GACHA...
HEY!
POPPA!
POP
POP
...SCATTERS CAPSULES FROM HIS BODY ONTO THE ROAD!
!
EEK!
WUP
WUP
WUP
WUP
THE CAPSULES ROLL STRAIGHT TOWARD THE CHECKMATE PAIR AND THE KID MUSCLE PAIR!
THE SUPERHUMANS BEHIND HIM CRASH INTO THE CAPSULES...
UGH!
...AND ARE KNOCKED INTO THE WALL!
AHH!
THK
UGH!
THK
WHOA!
DGG

CHECK-MATE TRANSFORMS HIMSELF INTO...
WUP WUP
WUP
...A KNIGHT!
FZZT
CLICK
CHESS PIECE CHANGE!
ZZZT
F
TOK
TOK
HE GALLOPS NIMBLY AROUND THE ROLLING CAPSULES!

WUP
WUP
WAAAH!
WHOA!

WUP
STOP! HELP! PLEASE!
WUP
W UP
YIKES!

THK
THK

VWP

HA!
DOOSH
OH! A CAPSULE FLIES OUT LIKE A BULLET!

HERE'S ANOTHER OF MY TRICKS!

THUK

HOW DO YOU LIKE--

NOTHING CAN HURT MY KNIGHT FORM!

SHOOM

OHH...

CHECKMATE LEAPS HIGH INTO THE AIR AND DODGES THE CAPSULE!

SHINYA!

UGH

SHINYA!
WHAT HAVE I DONE? I WAS SO FOCUSED ON DODGING THE CAPSULES...
...I FORGOT ABOUT SHINYA!

KING!
CLICK
CHANGE!

Z
Z

GET BACK IN THE RACE...
CH-CHECKMATE... G-GO AHEAD AND DRAG MY BODY...

AS A SUPER-HUMAN, I MUST CONSIDER THE LIFE AND SAFETY...
...OF HUMANS BEFORE MY OWN.

...

OH! CHECKMATE REMOVES THE BELT THAT BOUND HIM TO HIS PARTNER!

VWP...

AT THIS MOMENT, MONACO'S CHECKMATE HAS BEEN DIS-QUALIFIED!

HEH! NO NEED TO PLAY IT UP!

THE BOTTOM LINE IS, HE JUST COULDN'T CUT IT!

MR. GACHA'S NOT GONNA GET AWAY WITH THIS!

YOU KNOW, I'M GETTING ANGRY, TOO!

FSH
FSH
FSH
KLAK
KLAK
THE MANTARO PAIR MOVES AHEAD BY SWIMMING THROUGH THE SEA OF CAPSULES!
KLAK
UWAAAAH!
KID & YONE ATTACK!!
SHUK

CHAPTER 138:
THE FIRST TO THE FINALS!

THE MANTARO PAIR LANDS...

...A HEAVY FLYING TACKLE ON MR. GACHA'S GUT!

THE SUPERHUMANS APPEARING IN CHAPTERS 137 AND 138 WERE BASED ON THE IDEAS FROM THE FOLLOWING READERS:

YOSHIMI YOSHIKAWA (AGE 28)
FUJI KIMURA (AGE 27)
HIROKI NAKAJIMA (AGE 29)
SHINOBU MIYAMOTO (AGE 32)
RYOTA TAKAYAMA (AGE 25)
TELMON (AGE 23)
SHOUJI ICHIKAWA (AGE 20)
YUSUKE WATANABE (AGE 22)
MASAYUKI SAEGUSA (AGE 19)
FUMIHIKO ISHIZAWA (AGE 24)
RICHARD (AGE 23)
SHUICHI MURASAWA (AGE 24)
TOKKI MURASE (AGE 24)
KAZUYA TAKAHAMA (AGE 20)
TAKESHI YAGI (AGE 31)

GRP
THAT ALL YOU GUYS GOT?
WAAH!
BUT MR. GACHA IS UNFAZED! HE GRABS YONEO BY THE LEG!
YONEO! YOUR RIGHT LEG! STICK OUT YOUR RIGHT LEG!
L- LIKE THIS?
NOW SWING IT BACK AS HARD AS YOU CAN!
O... OKAY!
THE MANTARO PAIR UNLEASHES A FINISHING BLOW TO MR. GACHA'S FACE!
KID & YONE GUILLOTINE LARIAT!

YOW!
SHUK
MR. GACHA IS DOWN!
TUP
WHOA!
I- I COULD GET USED TO THIS!

...

CHECK-MATE...

VVP
NO MERCY TO THE DEFEATED!

WHEN YOU REACH THE TOP, ALLOW ME TO CHALLENGE YOU!
BUT DO NOT PITY ME! ADVANCE IN THE SUPER-HUMAN WORLD!
THAT KINDNESS, MANTARO... IT'S YOUR GREATEST VIRTUE.
B-BUT...

YOU READY, YONEO?
WUP
WUP
YES, SIR!
AND NOW THE MANTARO PAIR IS BACK IN THE RACE!
RIDING ON MR. GACHA'S CAPSULES...
WUP
WUP
WUP
WUP
...THEY OVERTAKE THE PAIR AHEAD OF THEM AT TREMENDOUS SPEED!

TAK
THEY'RE DOWN TO FOUR PAIRS!
TAK
TAK
THESE ARE THE LEAD RUNNERS!

THE HONOR OF FIRST PLACE BELONGS TO ME, KAISER MOON!

KA DAK
ENGLAND'S KEVIN MASK AND MALAYSIA'S KAISER MOON...
...TACKLE EACH OTHER FIERCELY!

LORD FLASH!

KEVIN MASK AND LORD FLASH SLIDE TOWARD KAISER MOON'S FEET!

!?

ZSSSH

WHOA!

KEVIN MASK SWEEPS KAISER MOON'S LEGS!

KAISER MOON TRIPS!

DOUBLE STUNNER!

SLAM

WVV
NW
DA!
EEK!
COMRADE TURBINSKI NOW TRIES A HIGH KICK AGAINST THE PAIR!
SHOOF
FWIP
BUT THE JAEGER PAIR ESCAPES IN THE NICK OF TIME!
...
WSSH

WAAA!

JAEGER STRIKES BACK AT THE COMRADE TURBINSKI PAIR!

YAAAH!

OO

WAIT!

BASH

TAK
WHILE JAEGER AND COMRADE TURBINSKI DUKE IT OUT...
TAK
...THE KEVIN MASK PAIR MAKES A FINAL DASH!

WE NOW TAKE YOU TO THE GOAL LINE IN ODAIBA'S KAIHIN PARK!
WAA
THOUSANDS OF FANS PACK THE STANDS, ANXIOUSLY WAITING TO SEE THE SUPERHUMANS CROSS THE LINE!
GOAL
SUPERHUMAN OLYMPICS THE RESURRECTION
SUPERHUMAN OLYMPICS
Fight!!
It's OK! Mr. No.1

THE CROWD ERUPTS AT THE SIGHT OF A SUPER-HUMAN ENTERING THE PARK!

WAA

GO GO COMRADE TURBINSKI

PRINCE MAN-TARO!

ROX-ANNE... I HOPE YOU'RE SAFE...

IT LOOKS LIKE THE KEVIN MASK PAIR IS FIRST!

WAA

TAK TAK

RIGHT BEHIND THEM ARE JAEGER AND COMRADE TURBINSKI!

GOAL
1
ENGLAND'S KEVIN MASK, THE FAVORITE TO WIN THE SUPER-HUMAN OLYMPICS ...
...LIVES UP TO THE HYPE AND FINISHES FIRST!
SUPERHUMAN OLYMPICS
FIGH
KEVIN! KEVIN!
KEV-IN!
KEVIN! KEVIN!
KEV-IN!
WAAA
HUMAN
OLYMPICS
1
HUMAN OLYMPICS
TMP
HE EARNS A SPOT IN THE GRAND FINALS!

TAK TAK TAK

I AIN'T LOSING TO NO GERMAN!

THE JAEGER PAIR AND THE COMRADE TURBINSKI PAIR ARE NECK AND NECK!

WHO WILL FINISH SECOND?

THIS IS UNBELIEVABLE! THE COMRADE TURBINSKI PAIR RUNS ON THE BRIDGE'S SUSPENSION CABLES!

KRANK KRANK KRANK

TAKING ADVANTAGE OF MEAT'S UNPARAL-LELED MIND...
TMP
...RUSSIA'S COMRADE TURBINSKI FINISHES SECOND!
SUPERHUMAN OLYMPICS
CLAP CLAP
CLAP
CLAP CLAP
CLAP CLAP
AND NOW, AMID HUGE APPLAUSE, GERMANY'S JAEGER APPROACHES IN THIRD PLACE!
WITH A HUMAN AS HIS PARTNER, A THIRD-PLACE FINISH IS NOTHING TO BE ASHAMED OF!
WE'RE ALMOST THERE, ROXANNE!

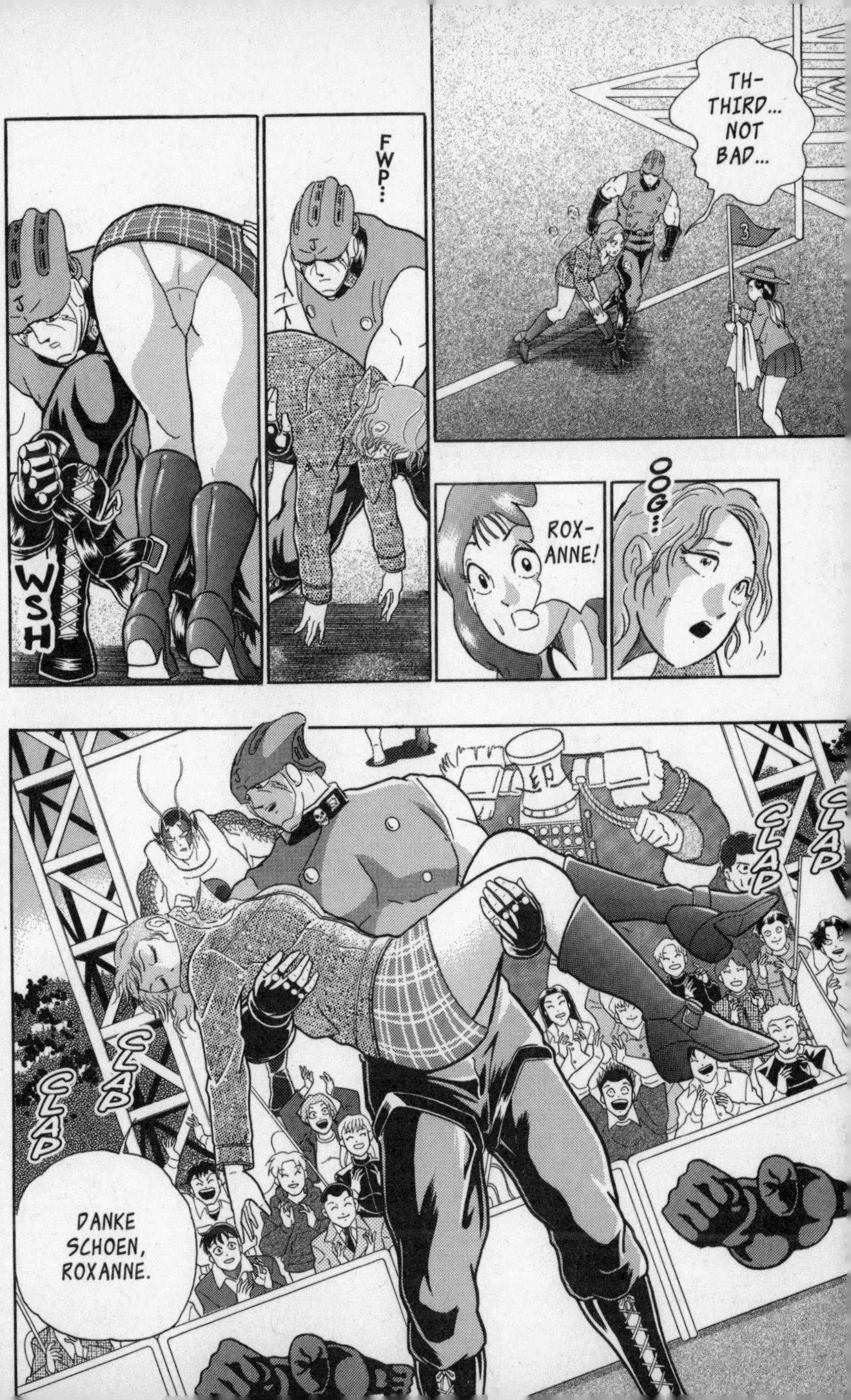

TH-THIRD... NOT BAD...

OOG...
ROX-ANNE!

FWP...

WSH

CLAP CLAP
DANKE SCHOEN, ROXANNE.
CLAP CLAP

THANKS, FOUR-EYES!
JUNIOR!
FWAP

MOVE! MOVE!
AUGH! I CAN'T STOP!
WUP
WUP
WUP
WUPPA
WAK
THERE'S A TURN COMING UP!
WE'RE GONNA CRASH!

OW!
OW!
...
LOOK, YONEO! THE RAINBOW BRIDGE!
WE PASSED A LOT OF FOLKS, BUT WHAT PLACE ARE WE IN?
YANK
STOP RIGHT THERE, MORONS!
WH-WHO ARE YOU?
SHUT YOUR MOUTH AND GET IN!
VSSH
WE'RE IN A HURRY! WHY DO WE HAVE TO GO FOR A RIDE?

HEH HEH! I'M UNDER ORDERS...

...TO STOP YOU TWO!

YIPE!

TO BE CONTINUED IN VOLUME 15!

COMING NEXT VOLUME...

The Superhuman Olympics preliminaries are giving Kid Muscle no end of trouble, and a wild ride with the Coasterman, a living roller coaster, isn't about to slow things down. But things really heat up at the main competition, where one bizarre superhuman after another prepares to take the Kid down. First up: Hollywood Bowl, who embodies all the fearsome power of...yes...a toilet! While Kid Muscle laughs it up, his chances of surviving the Superhuman Olympics spiral down the drain!

AVAILABLE IN NOVEMBER 2006!

SUBSCRIBE TODAY & BECOME
MEMBER OF THE SHONEN JUM
SUBSCRIBER CLUB...
You'll get:
*Access to Exclusive Online Content!
*50% Savings Off the Newsstand Price!
*Exclusive Premiums!
All this available ONLY to Subscribers!
SHONEN JUMP
THE WORLD'S MOST POPULAR MANGA
FILL OUT THE SUBSCRIPTION CARD ON THE OTHER SIDE, OR SUBSCRIBE ONLINE AT:
www.shonenjump.com